I0795477

Printed in the United States
by Baker & Taylor Publisher Services

באדוף בענטשער

Budoff Bencher

A Book of Prayers and Songs for a Messianic Jewish Home

Edited by
Rabbi Kirk Gliebe
ר׳ שאול בן־יוסף

First Edition: October 23, 2023
- 2nd Printing - May 22, 2025

Published and Distributed by:
Devar Emet Messianic Publications
7800 Niles Avenue; Skokie, IL 60077
847-674-9146
www.demjo.org

ISBN: 979-8-9878279-2-5

Cover art by Elisa Rudolph

Table of Contents:

Introduction to the Budoff Bencher

Jewish life begins and ends in the home, not in the synagogue. This should seem pretty obvious since Jewish people, like most people, spend most of their time in their homes eating, sleeping and just plain living. Because of this, Jewish people have developed a simple book, called a ***bentcher*** in Yiddish but commonly spelled ***bencher*** in English, that contains specific prayers, blessings and songs to enhance the spiritual, traditional and cultural lives of Jewish people within their homes.

This is a Messianic Jewish Bencher. It is very much like every other bencher you might have seen or used, except that it also speaks clearly of the supremacy of our Messiah, the Lord Yeshua. Whether we are entering or concluding Shabbat and Holidays in our homes, or reciting our thanks to God after we have eaten, this bencher honors Israel's Messiah within the traditions of the Jewish People as we observe these traditions in our homes with our families. It is my hope that this Budoff Bencher will encourage Jewish followers of Messiah Yeshua in their homes to develop a stronger faith in the God of Israel and practice a more committed traditional observance of Jewish life.

Rabbi Kirk Gliebe

Hebrew Transliteration Guide:

Hebrew Consonants	Transliteration	Sound
ח	ḥ (see dot below "h")	**Ch**anukah
ךְ,ך,כ	kh	Baru**kh**
ךּ,כּ	k	**K**ippah
שׁ	sh	**Sh**abbat
שׂ	s	**S**amuel
ץ,צ	ts	**Ts**'dakah
ה	h	**H**alleluyah

Hebrew Vowels	Transliteration	Sound
אָ	a	**Awe**
אַ	a	**A**pple
אִ	i	B**ee**
אֵ	ei	L**ay**
אֶ	e	B**e**d
אֹ or וֹ	o	R**o**w
אֻ or וּ	u	B**oot**
אְ	sometimes e or sometimes ' like b**e**d. When silent or ending a syllable its a '.	

Erev Shabbat Blessings & Kiddush

Traditional Candle Lighting Blessing for Shabbat

(After lighting at least two candles, the blessings are recited)

בָּרוּךְ אַתָּה יְיָ אֱלֹהֵינוּ מֶלֶךְ הָעוֹלָם, אֲשֶׁר קִדְּשָׁנוּ בְּמִצְוֹתָיו,
וְצִוָּנוּ לְהַדְלִיק נֵר שֶׁל שַׁבָּת.

Barukh atah Adonai Eloheinu Melekh Ha'Olam,
asher kid'shanu b'mitsvotav, v'tsivanu l'hadlik neir shel Shabbat.

Blessed are You, Lord our God, King of the Universe, who has sanctified us with His commandments, and commanded us to light the Shabbat lights.

Blessing in Remembrance of Messiah Yeshua

בָּרוּךְ אַתָּה יְיָ אֱלֹהֵינוּ מֶלֶךְ הָעוֹלָם, אֲשֶׁר קִדְּשָׁנוּ בִּדְבָרוֹ,
וְנָתַן לָנוּ אֶת יֵשׁוּעַ מְשִׁיחֵנוּ, וְצִוָּנוּ לִהְיוֹת אוֹר לָעוֹלָם.

Barukh atah Adonai Eloheinu Melekh Ha'Olam, asher kid'shanu bidvaro, v'natan lanu et Yeishua Meshiḥeinu, v'tsivanu l'hiyot or la'olam.

Blessed are You, Lord our God, King of the Universe, who has sanctified us with his word, and has given us Yeshua our Messiah, and commanded us to be light to the world.

Traditional Candle Lighting Blessing for Festivals

(After lighting at least two candles, the blessings are recited. Add words in parentheses on Shabbat. On Yom Kippur replace the regular word(s) for Festivals with the specific words for Yom Kippur in brackets)

בָּרוּךְ אַתָּה יְיָ אֱלֹהֵינוּ מֶלֶךְ הָעוֹלָם, אֲשֶׁר קִדְּשָׁנוּ בְּמִצְוֹתָיו,
וְצִוָּנוּ לְהַדְלִיק נֵר שֶׁל (שַׁבָּת וְשֶׁל) יוֹם טוֹב [יוֹם הַכִּפּוּרִים].

Barukh atah Adonai Eloheinu Melech Ha'Olam, asher kid'shanu b'mitsvotav v'tsivanu l'hadlik neir shel (Shabbat v'shel) Yom Tov [Yom HaKippurim].

Blessed are you, Lord our God, King of the Universe, who has sanctified us with His commandments, and commanded us to light the (Shabbat and) Holiday [Yom Kippur] lights.

(On very special occasions, recite the Sheheḥeyanu blessing)

בָּרוּךְ אַתָּה יְיָ אֱלֹהֵינוּ מֶלֶךְ הָעוֹלָם, שֶׁהֶחֱיָנוּ, וְקִיְּמָנוּ, וְהִגִּיעָנוּ, לַזְּמַן הַזֶּה.

Barukh atah Adonai Eloheinu Melekh Ha'Olam, sheheḥeyanu, vekiyemanu, vehigiyanu, lazman hazeh!

Blessed are You, Lord our God, King of the Universe, who has kept us, and sustained us, and enabled us to reach this season!

Shalom Aleikhem

שָׁלוֹם עֲלֵיכֶם, מַלְאֲכֵי הַשָּׁרֵת, מַלְאֲכֵי עֶלְיוֹן,
מִמֶּלֶךְ מַלְכֵי הַמְּלָכִים, הַקָּדוֹשׁ בָּרוּךְ הוּא.

Shalom aleikhem mal'akhei hashareit, mal'akhei Elyon,
mimelekh Malkhei ham'lakhim, Hakadosh barukh hu.

בּוֹאֲכֶם לְשָׁלוֹם, מַלְאֲכֵי הַשָּׁלוֹם, מַלְאֲכֵי עֶלְיוֹן,
מִמֶּלֶךְ מַלְכֵי הַמְּלָכִים, הַקָּדוֹשׁ בָּרוּךְ הוּא.

Boakhem l'shalom, mal'akhei hashalom, mal'akhei Elyon,
mimelekh Malkhei ham'lakhim, Hakadosh barukh hu.

בָּרְכוּנִי לְשָׁלוֹם, מַלְאֲכֵי הַשָּׁלוֹם, מַלְאֲכֵי עֶלְיוֹן,
מִמֶּלֶךְ מַלְכֵי הַמְּלָכִים, הַקָּדוֹשׁ בָּרוּךְ הוּא.

Barkhuni l'shalom, mal'akhei hashalom, mal'akhei Elyon,
mimelekh Malkhei ham'lakhim, Hakadosh barukh hu.

צֵאתְכֶם לְשָׁלוֹם, מַלְאֲכֵי הַשָּׁלוֹם, מַלְאֲכֵי עֶלְיוֹן,
מִמֶּלֶךְ מַלְכֵי הַמְּלָכִים, הַקָּדוֹשׁ בָּרוּךְ הוּא.

Tseitkhem l'shalom, mal'akhei hashalom, mal'akhei Elyon,
mimelekh Malkhei ham'lakhim, Hakadosh barukh hu.

Peace be unto you, messengers who serve; messengers of the Almighty,
the sovereign King of kings, the Holy One, blessed is He.
Come in peace, you messengers of peace, messengers of the Almighty,
the sovereign King of kings, the Holy One, blessed is He.
Bless us with peace, you messengers of peace, messengers of the
Almighty, the sovereign King of kings, blessed is He.
Leave us in peace, you messengers of peace, messengers of the
Almighty, the sovereign King of kings, blessed is He.

Eishet Ḥayil

(Proverbs 31 is read before the Kiddush by the husband to honor to his wife)

אֵשֶׁת חַיִל מִי יִמְצָא וְרָחֹק מִפְּנִינִים מִכְרָהּ. בָּטַח בָּהּ לֵב
בַּעְלָהּ וְשָׁלָל לֹא יֶחְסָר. גְּמָלַתְהוּ טוֹב וְלֹא־רָע כֹּל יְמֵי
חַיֶּיהָ. דָּרְשָׁה צֶמֶר וּפִשְׁתִּים וַתַּעַשׂ בְּחֵפֶץ כַּפֶּיהָ. הָיְתָה
כָּאֳנִיּוֹת סוֹחֵר מִמֶּרְחָק תָּבִיא לַחְמָהּ. וַתָּקָם בְּעוֹד לַיְלָה
וַתִּתֵּן טֶרֶף לְבֵיתָהּ וְחֹק לְנַעֲרֹתֶיהָ. זָמְמָה שָׂדֶה וַתִּקָּחֵהוּ
מִפְּרִי כַפֶּיהָ נָטְעָה כָּרֶם. חָגְרָה בְעוֹז מָתְנֶיהָ וַתְּאַמֵּץ
זְרוֹעֹתֶיהָ. טָעֲמָה כִּי־טוֹב סַחְרָהּ לֹא־יִכְבֶּה בַלַּיְלָה
נֵרָהּ. יָדֶיהָ שִׁלְּחָה בַכִּישׁוֹר וְכַפֶּיהָ תָּמְכוּ פָלֶךְ. כַּפָּהּ פָּרְשָׂה
לֶעָנִי וְיָדֶיהָ שִׁלְּחָה לָאֶבְיוֹן. לֹא־תִירָא לְבֵיתָהּ מִשָּׁלֶג כִּי
כָל־בֵּיתָהּ לָבֻשׁ שָׁנִים. מַרְבַדִּים עָשְׂתָה־לָּהּ שֵׁשׁ וְאַרְגָּמָן
לְבוּשָׁהּ. נוֹדָע בַּשְּׁעָרִים בַּעְלָהּ בְּשִׁבְתּוֹ עִם־זִקְנֵי־אָרֶץ. סָדִין
עָשְׂתָה וַתִּמְכֹּר וַחֲגוֹר נָתְנָה לַכְּנַעֲנִי. עֹז־וְהָדָר לְבוּשָׁהּ
וַתִּשְׂחַק לְיוֹם אַחֲרוֹן.

Eishet ḥayil mi yimtza v'raḥok mip'ninim mikhrah.
Bataḥ bah leiv ba'lah v'shalal lo yeḥsar.
G'malatu tov v'lo ra kol y'mei ḥa-yeyha.
Darshah tzemer ufishtim vata'as b'ḥeifetz kapeyha.
Haitah ka'a-niyot soḥeir mimerḥak tavi laḥmah.
Vatakom be'od lailah vatitein teref l'veitah v'ḥok l'na'aroteyha.
Zam'mah sadeh vatikaḥeihu mipri khapeyha nat'ah karem.
Ḥagrah v'oz mat'neyha vat'ameits zero'oteyha.
Ta'amah ki tov sah'rah lo yikhbeh ba'lailah neirah.
Yadeha shilḥah vakishor v'khapeyha tamkhu falekh.
Kapah parsah le'ani v'yadeha shil'ḥah la'evyon.
Lo tira l'veitah mishaleg ki khol beitah lavush shanim.
Marvadim as'tah lah sheish v'argaman l'vushah.
Noda bash'arim ba'lah b'shivto im ziknei arets.
Sadin astah vatimkor vaḥagor nat'nah lak'na'ani.
Oz v'hadar l'vushah vatisḥak l'yom aḥaron.

פִּיהָ פָּתְחָה בְחָכְמָה וְתוֹרַת־חֶסֶד עַל־לְשׁוֹנָהּ. צוֹפִיָּה
הֲלִיכוֹת בֵּיתָהּ וְלֶחֶם עַצְלוּת לֹא תֹאכֵל. קָמוּ בָנֶיהָ
וַיְאַשְּׁרוּהָ בַּעְלָהּ וַיְהַלְלָהּ. רַבּוֹת בָּנוֹת עָשׂוּ חָיִל וְאַתְּ עָלִית
עַל־כֻּלָּנָה. שֶׁקֶר הַחֵן וְהֶבֶל הַיֹּפִי אִשָּׁה יִרְאַת־יְיָ הִיא
תִתְהַלָּל. תְּנוּ־לָהּ מִפְּרִי יָדֶיהָ וִיהַלְלוּהָ בַשְּׁעָרִים מַעֲשֶׂיהָ.

Piha pat'ḥah v'ḥokhmah v'torat ḥesed al l'shonah.
Tsofi'ah halikhot bei'tah v'leḥem atslut lo tokheil.
Kamu vaneha vayash'ruha ba'lah vay'halelah.
Rabot banot asu ḥayil v'at aliyt al kulanah.
Sheker haḥein v'hevel hayofiy ishah yir'at Adonai hi tit'halal.
Tenu lah mip'ri yadeha vi-haleluha vash'arim ma'asehah.

A woman of valor, who can find? Her value is far beyond pearls. Her husband's heart relies on her and he shall lack no fortune. She does him good and not evil, all the days of her life. She seeks wool and flax, and works with her hands willingly. She is like the merchant ships in bringing her bread from afar. She gets up while it is still night, and gives food to her household and a portion to her maidservants. She plans for a field, and buys it. With the fruit of her hands she plants a vineyard. She girds her loins in strength, and makes her arms strong. She knows that her merchandise is good. Her candle does not go out at night. She sets her hands to the spindle, and holds the spinning wheel in her hands. She extends her hands to the poor, and reaches out her hand to the needy. She fears not for her household because of snow, because her whole household is warmly dressed. She makes covers for herself, her clothing is fine linen and purple. Her husband is known at the gates and he sits among the elders of the land. She makes a coat and sells it, and she delivers clothing to the merchant. Strength and honor are her clothing and she smiles at the future. She opens her mouth with wisdom, and kindness is on her tongue. She watches over the ways of her household, and does not eat the bread of idleness. Her children rise up and praise her, her husband lauds her, "Many women have acted in a worthy manner, but you surpass them all." Charm is deceptive and beauty is vain, but a woman who fears God shall be praised. Give her of the fruit of her hands, and let her works praise her in the gates.

Blessing the Children

(It is customary on Erev Shabbat for parents to bless their children, placing their hands on their children's heads and reciting the following blessing)

For Boys: יְשִׂמְךָ אֱלֹהִים כְּאֶפְרַיִם וְכִמְנַשֶּׁה.

Y'simkha Elohim k'Efrayim v'khi Menasheh.

May God make you like Ephraim and Manasseh.

For Girls: יְשִׂמֵךְ אֱלֹהִים כְּשָׂרָה רִבְקָה רָחֵל וְלֵאָה.

Yis'meikh Elohim k'Sara Rivka Raḥeil v'Lei'ah.

May God make you like Sarah, Rebekah, Rachel and Leah.

יְבָרֶכְךָ יְיָ וְיִשְׁמְרֶךָ.

Y'varekh'kha Adonai v'yishm'rekha.

יָאֵר יְיָ פָּנָיו אֵלֶיךָ וִיחֻנֶּךָּ.

Ya'eir Adonai panav eilekha viḥuneka.

יִשָּׂא יְיָ פָּנָיו אֵלֶיךָ וְיָשֵׂם לְךָ שָׁלוֹם.

Yisa Adonai panav eilekha v'yaseim l'kha shalom.

The Lord bless you and keep you!
The Lord make His face to shine upon you
and be gracious unto you!
The Lord turn His face unto you, and give you peace!

Matthew 19:13-14

אָז הֵבִיאוּ אֵלָיו יְלָדִים כְּדֵי שֶׁיִּסְמֹךְ יָדָיו עֲלֵיהֶם וְיִתְפַּלֵּל בַּעֲדָם, אֶלָּא שֶׁהַתַּלְמִידִים גָּעֲרוּ בָּהֶם. אַךְ יֵשׁוּעַ אָמַר: "הַנִּיחוּ לַיְלָדִים לָבוֹא אֵלַי וְאַל תִּמְנְעוּ בַּעֲדָם, כִּי לְכָאֵלֶּה מַלְכוּת הַשָּׁמַיִם." הוּא סָמַךְ יָדָיו עֲלֵיהֶם וְאַחֲרֵי כֵן הָלַךְ מִשָּׁם.

Then children were brought to him that he might lay his hands on them and pray. The talmidim rebuked the people, but Yeshua said, "Let the children come to me, and do not hinder them, for to them belongs the kingdom of heaven." And he laid his hands on them and went away.

Kiddush for Erev Shabbat

(Kiddush is recited over a full cup of wine or grape juice which is drunk after reciting the final blessing)

(Quietly : וַיְהִי עֶרֶב וַיְהִי בֹקֶר) יוֹם הַשִּׁשִּׁי. וַיְכֻלּוּ הַשָּׁמַיִם וְהָאָרֶץ וְכָל צְבָאָם. וַיְכַל אֱלֹהִים בַּיּוֹם הַשְּׁבִיעִי מְלַאכְתּוֹ אֲשֶׁר עָשָׂה, וַיִּשְׁבֹּת בַּיּוֹם הַשְּׁבִיעִי מִכָּל מְלַאכְתּוֹ אֲשֶׁר עָשָׂה. וַיְבָרֶךְ אֱלֹהִים אֶת יוֹם הַשְּׁבִיעִי וַיְקַדֵּשׁ אֹתוֹ, כִּי בוֹ שָׁבַת מִכָּל מְלַאכְתּוֹ אֲשֶׁר בָּרָא אֱלֹהִים לַעֲשׂוֹת.

(Quietly: *Vay'hi erev vay'hi voker) yom hashishi. Vay'khulu hashamayim v'ha'arets v'khol ts'va-am. Vay'khal Elohim bayom hashvi'i m'lakhto asher asah, va'yishbot bayom hashvi'i mikol melakhto asher asah. Vayevarekh Elohim et yom hashvi'i vay'kadeish otoh, ki vo shavat mikol melakh'to asher barah Elohim la'asot.*

בָּרוּךְ אַתָּה יְיָ אֱלֹהֵינוּ מֶלֶךְ הָעוֹלָם, בּוֹרֵא פְּרִי הַגָּפֶן.

Barukh atah Adonai Eloheinu Melekh Ha'Olam, borei p'ri ha'gafen.

בָּרוּךְ אַתָּה יְיָ אֱלֹהֵינוּ מֶלֶךְ הָעוֹלָם, אֲשֶׁר קִדְּשָׁנוּ בְּמִצְוֹתָיו וְרָצָה בָנוּ, וְשַׁבַּת קָדְשׁוֹ בְּאַהֲבָה וּבְרָצוֹן הִנְחִילָנוּ זִכָּרוֹן לְמַעֲשֵׂה בְרֵאשִׁית. כִּי הוּא יוֹם תְּחִלָּה לְמִקְרָאֵי קֹדֶשׁ, זֵכֶר לִיצִיאַת מִצְרָיִם. כִּי בָנוּ בָחַרְתָּ וְאוֹתָנוּ קִדַּשְׁתָּ, מִכָּל הָעַמִּים, וְשַׁבַּת קָדְשְׁךָ בְּאַהֲבָה וּבְרָצוֹן הִנְחַלְתָּנוּ.
בָּרוּךְ אַתָּה יְיָ, מְקַדֵּשׁ הַשַּׁבָּת.

Barukh atah Adonai Eloheinu Melekh Ha'Olam, asher kid'shanu b'mitsvotav v'ratsah vanu, v'shabbat kodsho b'ahavah uv'ratson hin'ḥilanu zikaron lema'aseih v'reishit. ki hoo yom t'ḥilah l'mikra'ei kodesh, zeikher l'tsi'at mits'rayim, ki vanu vaḥar'tah v'otanu kidash'ta mikol ha'amim, v'shabbat kodshekha b'ahavah uv'ratson hin'ḥaltanu. Barukh atah Adonai, m'kadeish ha'Shabbat.

(Quietly: And there was evening and there was morning) the sixth day. And thus the heavens, and the earth, and all their hosts were finished. And on the seventh day God completed all the work in which He had been engaged, and on the seventh day He rested from all the work which He had made. And God blessed the seventh day calling it holy, for on it He rested from all of the work which He had created.

Blessed are You, Lord our God, King of the Universe, who creates the fruit of the vine.

Blessed are You, Lord our God, King of the Universe, who was pleased with us, and who has set us apart with His commandments. In love and in favor He has given us His holy Shabbat as a part of our inheritance; a remembrance of the creation. The Shabbat is first among all the days of holy assembly to recall the exodus from Egypt. Surely You have chosen us; You have set us apart from all other peoples, and in love and favor You have given us Your holy Shabbat as an inheritance. Blessed are You, Lord, who has made the Shabbat holy.

(Drink the cup)

(Using a cup or traditional handwashing vessel, wash first the right hand, fully washing from the wrist down to the fingertips, then the left hand, alternating hands until both have been washed three times, then say the blessing. It is traditional not to speak after washing until one recites the Motsi)

Blessing for Washing Hands

בָּרוּךְ אַתָּה יְיָ אֱלֹהֵינוּ מֶלֶךְ הָעוֹלָם, אֲשֶׁר קִדְּשָׁנוּ בְּמִצְוֹתָיו, וְצִוָּנוּ עַל נְטִילַת יָדָיִם.

Barukh atah Adonai, Eloheinu Melekh Ha'Olam, asher kid'shanu b'mitsvotav, v'tsivanu al netilat yadayim.

Blessed are You, Lord our God, King of the Universe, who has sanctified us with His commandments and has commanded us regarding washing our hands.

Motsi

בָּרוּךְ אַתָּה יְיָ אֱלֹהֵינוּ מֶלֶךְ הָעוֹלָם, הַמּוֹצִיא לֶחֶם מִן הָאָרֶץ.

Barukh atah Adonai Eloheinu Melekh Ha'Olam, hamotsi leḥem min ha'arets.

Blessed are You, Lord our God, King of the Universe, who brings forth bread from the earth.

(Sprinkle salt on the challah before eating as a reminder of the salt that seasoned the Temple sacrifices)

John 6:35

אָמַר לָהֶם יֵשׁוּעַ: "אֲנִי הוּא לֶחֶם הַחַיִּים. כָּל הַבָּא אֵלַי לֹא יִרְעַב, וְהַמַּאֲמִין בִּי לֹא יִצְמָא עוֹד."

Yeshua said to them, "I am the bread of life. The person who comes to Me will not hunger, and the person who believes in Me will never thirst."

Kiddush for Shabbat & Festival Morning

(Kiddush is recited over a full cup of wine or grape juice which is drunk after reciting the final blessing. On a Festival which ***<u>is also a Shabbat,</u>*** *begin here)*

Isaiah 58:13-14

אִם־תָּשִׁיב מִשַּׁבָּת רַגְלֶךָ עֲשׂוֹת חֲפָצֶךָ בְּיוֹם קָדְשִׁי
וְקָרָאתָ לַשַּׁבָּת עֹנֶג לִקְדוֹשׁ יְיָ מְכֻבָּד וְכִבַּדְתּוֹ מֵעֲשׂוֹת
דְּרָכֶיךָ מִמְּצוֹא חֶפְצְךָ וְדַבֵּר דָּבָר. אָז תִּתְעַנַּג עַל־יְיָ
וְהִרְכַּבְתִּיךָ עַל־בָּמֳתֵי אָרֶץ וְהַאֲכַלְתִּיךָ נַחֲלַת יַעֲקֹב אָבִיךָ
כִּי פִּי יְיָ דִּבֵּר.

If you keep your foot from breaking the Shabbat, from pursuing your own pleasure on My holy day, and if you call the Shabbat a delight and the holy day of the Lord honorable, and honor it by not pursuing your own interests or pleasure, nor speaking your own words, then you will delight yourself in the Lord, and I will make you to ride upon the high places of the earth. I will feed you with the inheritance of Jacob your father, for the mouth of the Lord has spoken.

V'shamru

Exodus 31:16-17

וְשָׁמְרוּ בְנֵי יִשְׂרָאֵל אֶת הַשַּׁבָּת, לַעֲשׂוֹת אֶת הַשַּׁבָּת
לְדֹרֹתָם בְּרִית עוֹלָם. בֵּינִי וּבֵין בְּנֵי יִשְׂרָאֵל אוֹת הִיא
לְעֹלָם, כִּי שֵׁשֶׁת יָמִים עָשָׂה יְיָ אֶת הַשָּׁמַיִם וְאֶת הָאָרֶץ,
וּבַיּוֹם הַשְּׁבִיעִי שָׁבַת וַיִּנָּפַשׁ.

V'shamru v'nei Yisraeil et ha'Shabbat, la'asot et ha'Shabbat l'dorotam b'rit olam. Beini u'vein b'nei Yisraeil ot hi l'olam, ki sheishet yamim asah Adonai et hashamayim v'et ha'arets, uvayom hash'vii shavat vayi'nafash.

And the children of Israel will keep the Shabbat, observing the Shabbat to all generations as an everlasting covenant. It is a sign between Me and the children of Israel forever, for in six days the Lord made the heavens and the earth, and on the seventh day He ceased from work and He rested.

Exodus 20:8-11

זָכוֹר אֶת יוֹם הַשַּׁבָּת לְקַדְּשׁוֹ. שֵׁשֶׁת יָמִים תַּעֲבֹד וְעָשִׂיתָ כָּל מְלַאכְתֶּךָ. וְיוֹם הַשְּׁבִיעִי שַׁבָּת לַייָ אֱלֹהֶיךָ, לֹא תַעֲשֶׂה כָל מְלָאכָה, אַתָּה וּבִנְךָ וּבִתֶּךָ עַבְדְּךָ וַאֲמָתְךָ וּבְהֶמְתֶּךָ, וְגֵרְךָ אֲשֶׁר בִּשְׁעָרֶיךָ. כִּי שֵׁשֶׁת יָמִים עָשָׂה יְיָ אֶת הַשָּׁמַיִם וְאֶת הָאָרֶץ אֶת הַיָּם וְאֶת כָּל אֲשֶׁר בָּם, וַיָּנַח בַּיּוֹם הַשְּׁבִיעִי. עַל כֵּן בֵּרַךְ יְיָ אֶת יוֹם הַשַּׁבָּת וַיְקַדְּשֵׁהוּ.

Remember the Shabbat day, so that you keep it holy. For six days you will labor and do all your work, but the seventh day is the Shabbat of the Lord your God. You shall do no work on it; neither you, nor your son, nor your daughter, nor your male servant, nor your female servant, nor your cattle, nor the stranger who dwells within your gates. For in six days the Lord made the heavens and the earth, the sea, and all that is in them, and He rested on the seventh day. Therefore, the Lord blessed the Shabbat day and made it holy.

(Begin here on Festivals that do not begin on Shabbat)

וַיְדַבֵּר מֹשֶׁה אֶת מוֹעֲדֵי יְיָ אֶל בְּנֵי יִשְׂרָאֵל.

Vay'dabeir Moshe et Moa'dei Adonai el Bnei Yisraeil.

Moses announced the Lord's Festivals to the Children of Israel.

(Only on Rosh Hashanah add)

תִּקְעוּ בַחֹדֶשׁ שׁוֹפָר, בַּכֶּסֶה לְיוֹם חַגֵּנוּ. כִּי חֹק לְיִשְׂרָאֵל הוּא, מִשְׁפָּט לֵאלֹהֵי יַעֲקֹב.

Tiku vaḥodesh shofar, ba'keseh l'yom ḥageinu. kiy ḥok l'Yisraeil hu, mish'pat lei'lohei Ya'akov.

Sound the shofar at the new moon, at the designated time for the day of our festival. This is a statute for Israel, an ordinance of the God of Jacob.

בָּרוּךְ אַתָּה יְיָ אֱלֹהֵינוּ מֶלֶךְ הָעוֹלָם, בּוֹרֵא פְּרִי הַגָּפֶן.

Barukh atah Adonai Eloheinu Melekh Ha'Olam, borei p'ri ha'gafen.

Blessed are You, Lord our God, King of the Universe, who creates the fruit of the vine.

Kiddush for Festival Evening

(Kiddush is recited over a full cup of wine or grape juice which is drunk after reciting the final blessing. On a Festival Evening which ***is also an Erev Shabbat,*** *begin here and read the portions in parenthesis.* ***For Rosh Hashanah*** *turn to the Kiddush that follows on page 17)*

(Quietly: וַיְהִי עֶרֶב וַיְהִי בֹקֶר) יוֹם הַשִּׁשִּׁי. וַיְכֻלּוּ הַשָּׁמַיִם וְהָאָרֶץ וְכָל צְבָאָם. וַיְכַל אֱלֹהִים בַּיּוֹם הַשְּׁבִיעִי מְלַאכְתּוֹ אֲשֶׁר עָשָׂה, וַיִּשְׁבֹּת בַּיּוֹם הַשְּׁבִיעִי מִכָּל מְלַאכְתּוֹ אֲשֶׁר עָשָׂה. וַיְבָרֶךְ אֱלֹהִים אֶת יוֹם הַשְּׁבִיעִי וַיְקַדֵּשׁ אֹתוֹ, כִּי בוֹ שָׁבַת מִכָּל מְלַאכְתּוֹ, אֲשֶׁר בָּרָא אֱלֹהִים לַעֲשׂוֹת.

(Quietly: *Vay'hi erev vay'hi voker) yom hashishi. Vay'khulu hashamayim v'ha'arets v'khol ts'vaam. Vay'khal Elohim bayom hashvi'i m'lakhto asher asah, va'yishbot bayom hashvi'i mikol melakhto asher asah. Vayevarekh Elohim et yom hashvi'i vay'kadeish otoh, ki vo shavat mikol melakh'to asher barah Elohim la'asot.*

(quietly: And there was evening and there was morning) the sixth day. And thus the heavens, and the earth, and all their hosts were finished. And on the seventh day God completed all the work in which He had been engaged, and on the seventh day He rested from all the work which He had made. And God blessed the seventh day calling it holy, for on it He rested from all of the work which He had created.

(On a Festival that ***is not*** *a Shabbat begin here and omit portions in parenthesis)*

בָּרוּךְ אַתָּה יְיָ אֱלֹהֵינוּ מֶלֶךְ הָעוֹלָם, בּוֹרֵא פְּרִי הַגָּפֶן.

Barukh atah Adonai Eloheinu Melekh Ha'Olam, borei p'ri ha'gafen.

Blessed are You, Lord our God, King of the Universe, who creates the fruit of the vine.

בָּרוּךְ אַתָּה יְיָ אֱלֹהֵינוּ מֶלֶךְ הָעוֹלָם, אֲשֶׁר בָּחַר בָּנוּ מִכָּל עָם וְרוֹמְמָנוּ מִכָּל לָשׁוֹן, וְקִדְּשָׁנוּ בְּמִצְוֹתָיו. וַתִּתֶּן לָנוּ יְיָ אֱלֹהֵינוּ בְּאַהֲבָה (שַׁבָּתוֹת לִמְנוּחָה וּ) מוֹעֲדִים לְשִׂמְחָה, חַגִּים וּזְמַנִּים לְשָׂשׂוֹן, אֶת יוֹם (הַשַּׁבָּת הַזֶּה וְאֶת יוֹם)...

Barukh atah Adonai Eloheinu Melekh Ha'Olam, asher bahar banu mikol am v'rom'manu mikol lashon, v'kidshanu b'mitsvotayv. Vatiten lanu Adonai Eloheinu b'ahavah (shabbatot lim'nuhah u) moadim l'simhah, hagim u-z'manim l'sason, et yom (haShabbat hazeh v'et yom)...

Blessed are You, Lord our God, King of the Universe, who has chosen and exalted us above all nations, and has set us apart with your commandments. And You, Lord our God, have given us *(Shabbats for rest,)* holidays for gladness and festival seasons for joy, *(this Shabbat day and this day of)* ...

לְפֶסַח: חַג הַמַּצּוֹת הַזֶּה, זְמַן חֵרוּתֵנוּ,

On Pesah add: *Hag HaMatsot hazeh, zeman heiruteinu,*

The Festival of Matsah, our Festival of Freedom,

לְשָׁבֻעוֹת: חַג הַשָּׁבֻעוֹת הַזֶּה, זְמַן מַתַּן תּוֹרָתֵנוּ,

On Shavuot add: *Hag HaShavuot hazeh, zeman matan Torateinu,*

The Festival of Shavuot, our Festival of the Gift of the Torah,

לְסֻכּוֹת: חַג הַסֻּכּוֹת הַזֶּה, זְמַן שִׂמְחָתֵנוּ,

On Sukkot add: *Hag HaSukkot hazeh, zeman simhateinu,*

The Festival of Sukkot, our Festival of Rejoicing,

לִשְׁמִינִי עֲצֶרֶת: הַשְּׁמִינִי חַג הָעֲצֶרֶת הַזֶּה, זְמַן שִׂמְחָתֵנוּ,

On Shemini Atseret add: *HaSh'mini Hag Ha'atseret hazeh, zeman simhateinu,*

The Festival of Shemini Atseret, our Festival of Rejoicing,

(בְּאַהֲבָה) מִקְרָא קֹדֶשׁ, זֵכֶר לִיצִיאַת מִצְרָיִם.

(b'ahavah) mik'ra kodesh, zeikher litsiyat Mitsrayim.

(in love,) a holy assembly in remembrance of the exodus from Egypt.

כִּי בָנוּ בָחַרְתָּ וְאוֹתָנוּ קִדַּשְׁתָּ מִכָּל הָעַמִּים, (וְשַׁבָּת) וּמוֹעֲדֵי קָדְשֶׁךָ (בְּאַהֲבָה וּבְרָצוֹן) בְּשִׂמְחָה וּבְשָׂשׂוֹן הִנְחַלְתָּנוּ.

Ki vanu vahar'tah v'otanu kidash'ta mikol ha'amim, (v'Shabbat) u'moadei kad'shekha (b'ahavah uv'ratson) b'simhah u'besason hin'haltanu.

Surely You have chosen and set us apart from all other peoples, *(and Shabbat)* and the holy Festivals *(in love and in favor)* you have given us in happiness and joy.

בָּרוּךְ אַתָּה יְיָ, מְקַדֵּשׁ (הַשַּׁבָּת וְ) יִשְׂרָאֵל וְהַזְּמַנִּים.

Barukh atah Adonai, m'kadeish (haShabbat v') Yisraeil v'hazemanim.

Blessed are You, Lord, who makes holy *(the Shabbat,)* Israel and the Festivals.

(If the Festival begins on Motsei Shabbat, continue by reciting the following for Havdalah over the already lit Festival candles, which are not to be extinguished)

בָּרוּךְ אַתָּה יְיָ אֱלֹהֵינוּ מֶלֶךְ הָעוֹלָם, בּוֹרֵא מְאוֹרֵי הָאֵשׁ. בָּרוּךְ אַתָּה יְיָ, אֱלֹהֵינוּ מֶלֶךְ הָעוֹלָם, הַמַּבְדִּיל בֵּין קֹדֶשׁ לְחוֹל, בֵּין אוֹר לְחֹשֶׁךְ, בֵּין יִשְׂרָאֵל לָעַמִּים, בֵּין יוֹם הַשְּׁבִיעִי לְשֵׁשֶׁת יְמֵי הַמַּעֲשֶׂה. בֵּין קְדֻשַּׁת שַׁבָּת לִקְדֻשַּׁת יוֹם טוֹב הִבְדַּלְתָּ, וְאֶת יוֹם הַשְּׁבִיעִי מִשֵּׁשֶׁת יְמֵי הַמַּעֲשֶׂה קִדַּשְׁתָּ. הִבְדַּלְתָּ וְקִדַּשְׁתָּ אֶת עַמְּךָ יִשְׂרָאֵל בִּקְדֻשָּׁתֶךָ. בָּרוּךְ אַתָּה יְיָ, הַמַּבְדִּיל בֵּין קֹדֶשׁ לְקֹדֶשׁ.

Barukh atah Adonai Eloheinu Melekh Ha'Olam, borei me'orei ha'eish. Barukh atah Adonai Eloheinu Melekh Ha'Olam, hamav'dil bein kodesh l'hol, bein ohr l'hoshekh, bein Yisraeil la'amim, bein yom hashvi'i, l'sheshet y'mei hama'aseh. Bein k'dushat shabbat lik'dushat yom tov hiv'daltah, v'et yom hash'vi-i mi'sheishet y'mei hama'aseh kidash'ta. Hiv'daltah v'kidashta et am'kha Yisraeil bik'dushatekha. Barukh atah Adonai, hamav'dil bein kodesh l'kodesh.

Blessed are You, Lord our God, King of the Universe, who creates the light of the fire. Blessed are You, Lord our God, for You have made a distinction between that which is holy and that which is common; between light and darkness; between Israel and the other nations; between the seventh day and the six days of work; between the sanctity of the Shabbat and the sanctity of the Festivals, distinguishing the sanctity of the seventh day from the six days of labor. You have set apart Israel Your people with Your holiness. Blessed are You, Lord, who has made a distinction between the holy and the profane.

(On the first night of Festivals recite the Sheheheyanu blessing)

בָּרוּךְ אַתָּה יְיָ אֱלֹהֵינוּ מֶלֶךְ הָעוֹלָם, שֶׁהֶחֱיָנוּ, וְקִיְּמָנוּ, וְהִגִּיעָנוּ, לַזְּמַן הַזֶּה.

Barukh atah Adonai, Eloheinu Melekh Ha'Olam, sheheḥeyanu, vekiyemanu, vehigiyanu, lazman hazeh.

Blessed are You, Lord our God, King of the Universe, who has kept us, and sustained us, and enabled us to reach this season!

(On Sukkot add the following if residing within a sukkah)

בָּרוּךְ אַתָּה יְיָ אֱלֹהֵינוּ מֶלֶךְ הָעוֹלָם, אֲשֶׁר קִדְּשָׁנוּ בְּמִצְוֹתָיו וְצִוָּנוּ לֵישֵׁב בַּסֻּכָּה.

Barukh atah Adonai, Eloheinu Melekh Ha'Olam, asher kid'shanu b'mitzvotayv v'tzivanu lei'yosheiv basukkah.

Blessed are You, Lord our God, King of the Universe, who has sanctified us with His commandments and has commanded us to dwell in a sukkah.

Kiddush for Erev Rosh Hashanah

(Kiddush is recited over a full cup of wine or grape juice which is drunk after reciting the final blessing. On a Rosh Hashanah Evening which ***is also an Erev Shabbat*** *begin here and read the portions in parenthesis)*

(Quietly : וַיְהִי עֶרֶב וַיְהִי בֹקֶר) יוֹם הַשִּׁשִּׁי. וַיְכֻלּוּ הַשָּׁמַיִם וְהָאָרֶץ
וְכָל צְבָאָם. וַיְכַל אֱלֹהִים בַּיּוֹם הַשְּׁבִיעִי מְלַאכְתּוֹ אֲשֶׁר
עָשָׂה, וַיִּשְׁבֹּת בַּיּוֹם הַשְּׁבִיעִי מִכָּל מְלַאכְתּוֹ אֲשֶׁר עָשָׂה.
וַיְבָרֶךְ אֱלֹהִים אֶת יוֹם הַשְּׁבִיעִי וַיְקַדֵּשׁ אֹתוֹ, כִּי בוֹ שָׁבַת
מִכָּל מְלַאכְתּוֹ, אֲשֶׁר בָּרָא אֱלֹהִים לַעֲשׂוֹת.

(Quietly: *Vay'hi erev vay'hi voker) yom hashishi. Vay'khulu hashamayim v'ha'arets v'khol ts'va-am. Vay'khal Elohim bayom hashvi'i m'lakhto asher asah, va'yishbot bayom hashvi'i mikol melakhto asher asah. Vayevarekh Elohim et yom hashvi'i vay'kadeish otoh, ki vo shavat mikol melakh'to asher barah Elohim la'asot.*

(quietly: And there was evening and there was morning) the sixth day. And thus the heavens, and the earth, and all their hosts were finished. And on the seventh day God completed all the work in which He had been engaged, and on the seventh day He rested from all the work which He had made. And God blessed the seventh day calling it holy, for on it He rested from all of the work which He had created.

(On a Rosh Hashanah Evening that ***is not an Erev Shabbat*** *begin here and omit portions in parenthesis)*

בָּרוּךְ אַתָּה יְיָ אֱלֹהֵינוּ מֶלֶךְ הָעוֹלָם, בּוֹרֵא פְּרִי הַגָּפֶן.

Barukh atah Adonai Eloheinu Melekh Ha'Olam, borei p'ri ha'gafen.

Blessed are You, Lord our God, King of the Universe, who creates the fruit of the vine.

בָּרוּךְ אַתָּה יְיָ אֱלֹהֵינוּ מֶלֶךְ הָעוֹלָם, אֲשֶׁר בָּחַר בָּנוּ מִכָּל עָם וְרוֹמְמָנוּ מִכָּל לָשׁוֹן, וְקִדְּשָׁנוּ בְּמִצְוֹתָיו. וַתִּתֶּן־לָנוּ יְיָ אֱלֹהֵינוּ בְּאַהֲבָה אֶת (יוֹם הַשַּׁבָּת הַזֶּה וְאֶת) יוֹם הַזִּכָּרוֹן הַזֶּה, יוֹם (זִכְרוֹן) תְּרוּעָה, (בְּאַהֲבָה) מִקְרָא קֹדֶשׁ, זֵכֶר לִיצִיאַת מִצְרָיִם

Barukh atah Adonai Eloheinu Melekh Ha'Olam, asher baḥar banu mikol am v'rom'manu mikol lashon, v'kidshanu b'mitsvotayv. Vatiten lanu Adonai Eloheinu b'ahavah et (yom haShabbat hazeh v'et) Yom HaZikaron hazeh, yom (zikron) t'ruah, (b'ahavah) mik'ra kodesh, zeikher litsiyat Mitsrayim.

Blessed are You, Lord our God, King of the Universe, who has chosen and exalted us above all nations, and has set us apart with your commandments. And You, Lord our God, have lovingly given us *(this Shabbat and)* this Day of Remembrance, a day for *(remembering)* the sound of the shofar, *(in love,)* a holy assembly in remembrance of the exodus from Egypt.

כִּי בָנוּ בָחַרְתָּ, וְאוֹתָנוּ קִדַּשְׁתָּ מִכָּל הָעַמִּים, וּדְבָרְךָ אֱמֶת וְקַיָּם לָעַד. בָּרוּךְ אַתָּה יְיָ, מֶלֶךְ עַל כָּל הָאָרֶץ, מְקַדֵּשׁ (הַשַּׁבָּת וְ) יִשְׂרָאֵל וְיוֹם הַזִּכָּרוֹן.

Ki vanu vaḥar'tah, v'otanu kidash'ta mikol ha'amim, u'devar'kha emet v'kayam la'ad. Barukh atah Adonai, melekh al kal ha'arets, m'kadeish (haShabbat v') Yisraeil v'Yom HaZikaron.

Surely You have chosen and set us apart from all other peoples, *(and Shabbat)* and the holy Festivals *(in love and in favor)* you have given us in happiness and joy. Blessed are You, Lord, who makes holy *(the Shabbat,)* Israel and the Festivals.

*(**If celebrating a second night of Rosh Hashanah** that coincides with Motsei Shabbat, continue by reciting the following for Havdalah over the already lit Festival candles, which are not to be extinguished)*

בָּרוּךְ אַתָּה יְיָ אֱלֹהֵינוּ מֶלֶךְ הָעוֹלָם, בּוֹרֵא מְאוֹרֵי הָאֵשׁ.
בָּרוּךְ אַתָּה יְיָ, אֱלֹהֵינוּ מֶלֶךְ הָעוֹלָם, הַמַּבְדִּיל בֵּין קֹדֶשׁ
לְחוֹל, בֵּין אוֹר לְחֹשֶׁךְ, בֵּין יִשְׂרָאֵל לָעַמִּים, בֵּין יוֹם
הַשְּׁבִיעִי לְשֵׁשֶׁת יְמֵי הַמַּעֲשֶׂה. בֵּין קְדֻשַּׁת שַׁבָּת לִקְדֻשַּׁת
יוֹם טוֹב הִבְדַּלְתָּ, וְאֶת יוֹם הַשְּׁבִיעִי מִשֵּׁשֶׁת יְמֵי הַמַּעֲשֶׂה
קִדַּשְׁתָּ. הִבְדַּלְתָּ וְקִדַּשְׁתָּ אֶת עַמְּךָ יִשְׂרָאֵל בִּקְדֻשָּׁתֶךָ.
בָּרוּךְ אַתָּה יְיָ, הַמַּבְדִּיל בֵּין קֹדֶשׁ לְקֹדֶשׁ.

Barukh atah Adonai Eloheinu Melekh Ha'Olam, borei me'orei ha'eish. Barukh atah Adonai Eloheinu Melekh Ha'Olam, hamav'dil bein kodesh l'ḥol, bein ohr l'ḥoshekh, bein Yisraeil la'amim, bein yom hashvi'i, l'sheshet y'mei hama'aseh. Bein k'dushat shabbat lik'dushat yom tov hiv'daltah. V'et yom hash'vi-i mi'sheishet y'mei hama'aseh kidash'ta. Hiv'daltah v'kidashta et am'kha Yisraeil bik'dushatekha.
Barukh atah Adonai, hamav'dil bein kodesh l'kodesh.

Blessed are You, Lord our God, King of the Universe, who creates the light of the fire. Blessed are You, Lord our God, for You have made a distinction between that which is holy and that which is common; between light and darkness; between Israel and the other nations; between the seventh day and the six days of work. Between the sanctity of the Shabbat and the sanctity of the Festivals, distinguishing the sanctity of the seventh day from the six days of labor. You have set apart Israel Your people with Your holiness. Blessed are You, Lord, who has made a distinction between one holy day and another.

(After the kiddush, on the first night of Rosh Hashanah recite the Sheheheyanu blessing)

בָּרוּךְ אַתָּה יְיָ אֱלֹהֵינוּ מֶלֶךְ הָעוֹלָם, שֶׁהֶחֱיָנוּ, וְקִיְּמָנוּ, וְהִגִּיעָנוּ, לַזְּמַן הַזֶּה.

Barukh atah Adonai Eloheinu Melekh Ha'Olam, sheheḥeyanu, vekiyemanu, vehigiyanu, lazman hazeh.

Blessed are You, Lord our God, King of the Universe, who has kept us, and sustained us, and enabled us to reach this season!

(After the kiddush, it is customary on Rosh Hashanah to eat a piece of apple dipped in honey as an expression of our hope for a sweet New Year and to recite the following blessings)

בָּרוּךְ אַתָּה יְיָ אֱלֹהֵינוּ מֶלֶךְ הָעוֹלָם בּוֹרֵא פְּרִי הָעֵץ.

Barukh atah Adonai Eloheinu Melekh Ha'Olam borei p'ri ha'eits.

Blessed are You, Lord our God, King of the Universe who creates the fruit of the tree.

יְהִי רָצוֹן מִלְּפָנֶיךָ יְיָ אֱלֹהֵינוּ וֵאלֹהֵי אֲבוֹתֵינוּ, שֶׁתְּחַדֵּשׁ עָלֵינוּ שָׁנָה טוֹבָה וּמְתוּקָה.

Yehi ratzon milfanekha Adonai Eloheinu vei'lohei avoteinu, shet'ḥadeish aleinu shanah tovah u'metukah.

May it be Your will, Lord our God and God of our fathers, to give to us a good and sweet new year.

Remembering the Death of Messiah Yeshua

(The following is recited in a spirit of quiet, self-examination)

1 Corinthians 10:16-17

כּוֹס הַבְּרָכָה שֶׁאָנוּ מְבָרְכִים עָלֶיהָ, הַאֵין הִיא הִתְחַבְּרוּת
לְדַם הַמָּשִׁיחַ. הַלֶּחֶם שֶׁאָנוּ בּוֹצְעִים, הַאֵין הוּא הִתְחַבְּרוּת
לְגוּף הַמָּשִׁיחַ. מִשּׁוּם שֶׁהַלֶּחֶם אֶחָד, אֲנַחְנוּ הָרַבִּים גּוּף
אֶחָד; שֶׁכֵּן כֻּלָּנוּ מִשְׁתַּתְּפִים בַּלֶּחֶם הָאֶחָד.

The cup of blessing which we bless, is it not our participation together of the blood atonement of the Messiah? The bread which we break, is it not our participation together of the bodily sacrifice of the Messiah? Because there is one bread, we who are many are united together in one community, for we all partake of the one bread.

1 Corinthians 11:23-29

אָכֵן אֲנִי קִבַּלְתִּי מֵאֵת הָאָדוֹן אֶת אֲשֶׁר גַּם מָסַרְתִּי לָכֶם.
שֶׁהָאָדוֹן יֵשׁוּעַ, בַּלַּיְלָה שֶׁהֻסְגַּר בּוֹ, לָקַח אֶת הַלֶּחֶם, בֵּרֵךְ,
בָּצַע אוֹתוֹ וְאָמַר. זֶה גּוּפִי הַנִּבְצָע בַּעַדְכֶם, זֹאת עֲשׂוּ
לְזִכְרִי. כֵּן גַּם לָקַח אֶת הַכּוֹס לְאַחַר הַסְּעוּדָה וְאָמַר. הַכּוֹס
הַזֹּאת הִיא הַבְּרִית הַחֲדָשָׁה בְּדָמִי, זֹאת עֲשׂוּ לְזִכְרִי בְּכָל
עֵת שֶׁתִּשְׁתּוּ. הֵן בְּכָל עֵת שֶׁאַתֶּם אוֹכְלִים אֶת הַלֶּחֶם הַזֶּה
וְשׁוֹתִים מִן הַכּוֹס הַזֹּאת, אַתֶּם מַזְכִּירִים אֶת מוֹת אֲדוֹנֵנוּ,
עַד שֶׁיָּבוֹא. לָכֵן מִי שֶׁאוֹכֵל מֵהַלֶּחֶם הַזֶּה אוֹ שׁוֹתֶה מִכּוֹס
הָאָדוֹן שֶׁלֹּא כָּרָאוּי, יִהְיֶה אָשֵׁם לְגַבֵּי גּוּף הָאָדוֹן וְדָמוֹ.
יִבְחַן נָא אִישׁ אֶת עַצְמוֹ וְכָךְ יֹאכַל מִן הַלֶּחֶם וְיִשְׁתֶּה מִן
הַכּוֹס, כִּי הָאוֹכֵל וְהַשּׁוֹתֶה מִבְּלִי לִנְהֹג הַבְחָנָה בְּגוּף הָאָדוֹן,
אוֹכֵל וְשׁוֹתֶה דִּין לְעַצְמוֹ.

For I received from the Lord that which also I delivered to you, that the Lord Yeshua during the night in which He was betrayed took bread, and when He had given thanks, He broke it, and said, “This is My body, which is given for you: do this in remembrance of Me." In the same way He took also the cup, after the meal, saying, "This cup is the New Covenant in My blood. This do, as often as you drink it, in remembrance of Me." For as often as you eat this bread, and drink this cup, you proclaim the Lord's death till He returns. Whoever eats the bread or drinks the cup of the Lord in an unworthy manner, will be guilty of the body and the blood of the Lord. But let a person examine themself, and then after this examination eat of the bread and drink of the cup. For the person who eats and drinks, eats and drinks judgment unto themself, if done so carelessly, not respecting Messiah's body.

John 6:35, 48-51

אָמַר לָהֶם יֵשׁוּעַ: אֲנִי הוּא לֶחֶם הַחַיִּים. כָּל הַבָּא אֵלַי לֹא
יִרְעַב, וְהַמַּאֲמִין בִּי לֹא יִצְמָא עוֹד. אֲנִי הוּא לֶחֶם הַחַיִּים.
אֲבוֹתֵיכֶם אָכְלוּ אֶת הַמָּן בַּמִּדְבָּר וָמֵתוּ. זֶה הוּא הַלֶּחֶם
הַיּוֹרֵד מִן הַשָּׁמַיִם כְּדֵי שֶׁיֹּאכְלוּ מִמֶּנּוּ וְלֹא יָמוּתוּ. אֲנִי
הַלֶּחֶם הַחַי הַיּוֹרֵד מִן הַשָּׁמַיִם. אִם יֹאכַל אִישׁ מִן הַלֶּחֶם הַזֶּה
יִחְיֶה לְעוֹלָם. וְהַלֶּחֶם אֲשֶׁר אֶתֵּן הֲרֵיהוּ בְּשָׂרִי בְּעַד חַיֵּי שֶׁל
הָעוֹלָם.

Yeshua said to them, "I am the bread of life. The person who comes to Me will not hunger, and the person who believes in Me will never thirst. I am the bread of life. Your fathers ate the manna in the wilderness, and they died. This is the bread which came down out of heaven, that a person may eat and not die. I am the living bread which came down out of heaven. If any person will eat of this bread, he shall live forever. The bread which I will give is My body, for the life of the world."

(Recite as a Statement of Personal Faith in Messiah Yeshua's Atonement)

יֵשׁוּעַ הַמָּשִׁיחַ תְּמוּרָתִי; יֵשׁוּעַ הַמָּשִׁיחַ מֵת כְּדֵי לְכַפֵּר עַל חֲטָאַי. דַּרְכּוֹ בִּלְבַד אֲנִי אֵלֵךְ לְחַיִּים טוֹבִים עִם אֱלֹהִים בְּשָׁלוֹם.

Yeishua HaMashiaḥ t'murati; Yeishua HaMashiaḥ meit kh'deiy l'kha-feir al ḥatay. Dar'ko vil'vad ani eileikh l'ḥay-yim tovim im Elohim v'shalom.

Messiah Yeshua is my exchange; Messiah Yeshua is my substitute, dying for the atonement of my sins. By His atonement alone am I able to be in relationship with God in peace.

Motsi

בָּרוּךְ אַתָּה יְיָ אֱלֹהֵינוּ מֶלֶךְ הָעוֹלָם, הַמּוֹצִיא לֶחֶם מִן הָאָרֶץ.

Barukh atah Adonai Eloheinu Melekh Ha'Olam, hamotsi leḥem min ha'arets.

Blessed are You, Lord our God, King of the Universe, who brings forth bread from the earth.

Remembering Messiah's Body

בָּרוּךְ אַתָּה יְיָ אֱלֹהֵינוּ מֶלֶךְ הָעוֹלָם, אֲשֶׁר קִדְּשָׁנוּ בְּמִצְוֹתָיו, וְצִוָּנוּ לִזְכּוֹר הַלֶּחֶם הַחַי, מְשִׁיחֵנוּ יֵשׁוּעַ.

Barukh atah Adonai Eloheinu Melekh Ha'Olam, asher kid'shanu b'mitsvotav, v'tsivanu liz'kor HaLeḥem HaḤai, Meshiḥeinu Yeishua.

Blessed are You, Lord our God, King of the Universe, who sanctifies us by His commandments and has commanded us to remember the Bread of Life, our Messiah Yeshua.

(Eat a piece of bread the size of an olive while soberly reflecting on Messiah Yeshua's death)

Avinu

**אָבִינוּ שֶׁבַּשָּׁמַיִם יִתְקַדֵּשׁ שְׁמֶךָ. תָּבֹא מַלְכוּתֶךָ יֵעָשֶׂה
רְצוֹנְךָ בָּאָרֶץ כַּאֲשֶׁר נַעֲשָׂה בַשָּׁמָיִם. תֶּן לָנוּ הַיּוֹם לֶחֶם
חֻקֵּנוּ. וּסְלַח לָנוּ אֶת אַשְׁמָתֵנוּ כַּאֲשֶׁר סֹלְחִים אֲנַחְנוּ
לַאֲשֶׁר אָשְׁמוּ לָנוּ. וְאַל תְּבִיאֵנוּ לִידֵי מַסָּה כִּי אִם הַצִּילֵנוּ
מִן הָרָע. כִּי לְךָ הַמַּמְלָכָה וְהַגְּבוּרָה וְהַתִּפְאֶרֶת לְעוֹלְמֵי
עוֹלָמִים.**

Avinu she'bashamayim yit'kadash sh'mekha. Tavo mal'khutekha ya'ase ritson'kha ba'arets ka'asher na'asah ba'shamayim. Ten lanu hayom leḥem ḥu'keinu. Us'laḥ lanu et ash'ma-teinu ka'asher sol'ḥim anaḥ'nu la'asher ash'mu lanu. V'al t'vi'einu lidei masah ki im hatsileinu min ha'rah. Ki l'kha ha-mam'lakhah v'hag'vurah v'hatiferet l'olimei olamim.

Our Father in Heaven, holy is Your name. Your kingdom will come; Your will shall be done, on the earth as it is in the heavens. Give us this day our daily bread. Forgive us our debts as we forgive our debtors. And lead us not into temptation, but deliver us from the evil one. For Yours is the kingdom, and the power, and the glory, forever.

Kiddush

בָּרוּךְ אַתָּה יְיָ, אֱלֹהֵינוּ מֶלֶךְ הָעוֹלָם, בּוֹרֵא פְּרִי הַגָּפֶן.

Barukh atah Adonai Eloheinu Melekh Ha'Olam, borei p'ri ha'gafen.

Blessed are You, Lord our God, King of the Universe, who creates the fruit of the vine.

Remembering Messiah's Blood

בָּרוּךְ אַתָּה יְיָ אֱלֹהֵינוּ מֶלֶךְ הָעוֹלָם, אֲשֶׁר קִדְּשָׁנוּ בְּמִצְוֹתָיו, וְצִוָּנוּ לִזְכּוֹר דָּם הַבְּרִית מְשִׁיחֵנוּ יֵשׁוּעַ.

Barukh atah Adonai, Eloheinu Melekh Ha'Olam, asher kid'shanu b'mitsvotav, v'tsivanu liz'kor Dam HaBrit Meshiḥeinu Yeishua.

Blessed are You, Lord our God, King of the Universe, who has commanded us to remember the Covenant Blood of our Messiah Yeshua.

(Drink a small cup of wine or grape juice while soberly reflecting on Messiah Yeshua's death)

Ephesians 4:1-7

לְפִיכָךְ אֲנִי, הָאָסִיר לְמַעַן הָאָדוֹן, מַפְצִיר בָּכֶם לְהִתְנַהֵג כַּיָּאֶה לַיִּעוּד שֶׁנִּקְרֵאתֶם אֵלָיו. הִתְנַהֲגוּ בְּכָל עֲנָוָה וּנְמִיכוּת רוּחַ, וּבְאֹרֶךְ אַפַּיִם. סִבְלוּ אִישׁ אֶת רֵעֵהוּ בְּאַהֲבָה. שִׁקְדוּ לִשְׁמֹר אֶת אַחְדוּת הָרוּחַ בְּקֶשֶׁר שֶׁל שָׁלוֹם. הִנֵּה, גּוּף אֶחָד וְרוּחַ אַחַת, כְּשֵׁם שֶׁגַּם אַתֶּם נִקְרֵאתֶם אֶל תִּקְוַת יִעוּדְכֶם הָאַחַת: אָדוֹן אֶחָד, אֱמוּנָה אַחַת, טְבִילָה אַחַת, אֵל וְאָב אֶחָד לַכֹּל, הוּא אֲשֶׁר מֵעַל כֹּל, פּוֹעֵל בַּכֹּל, וּבְתוֹךְ הַכֹּל. אֲבָל לְכָל אֶחָד וְאֶחָד מֵאִתָּנוּ הֻעֲנַק חֶסֶד כְּפִי הַמִּדָּה שֶׁהֶעֱנִיק לוֹ הַמָּשִׁיחַ.

I therefore, the prisoner of the Lord, plead with you to walk worthy of the calling to which you were called, with all humility and meekness, with patience, putting up with one another in love; working hard to keep the unity of the Spirit in the bond of peace.

There is one Body, and one Spirit, even as you also were called in one hope of your calling: one Lord, one faith, one immersion, one God and Father of all, who is over all, and through all, and in all. But to each one of us has been given the special enablement needed according to the grace of Messiah.

Hebrews 12:1-2

לָכֵן גַּם אֲנַחְנוּ, אֲשֶׁר עֲנַן עֵדִים כָּזֶה אוֹפֵף אוֹתָנוּ, נָסִירָה
נָא כָּל מַעֲמָסָה וְגַם אֶת הַחֵטְא הַלּוֹכֵד עַל נְקַלָּה,
וּבְסַבְלָנוּת נָרוּצָה אֶת הַמֵּרוֹץ הֶעָרוּךְ לְפָנֵינוּ, בְּהַבִּיטֵנוּ אֶל
יֵשׁוּעַ מְכוֹנֵן הָאֱמוּנָה וּמַשְׁלִימָהּ, אֲשֶׁר בְּעַד הַשִּׂמְחָה
הָעֲרוּכָה לְפָנָיו סָבַל אֶת הַצְּלָב וּבָז לַחֶרְפָּה, וַיֵּשֶׁב לִימִין
כִּסֵּא הָאֱלֹהִים.

Because of this, seeing that we are surrounded with so great a cloud of witnesses, let us also set aside every distraction and the sin which so easily trips us up, and let us run with endurance the race that is set before us, keeping our eyes fixed on Yeshua who is the author and perfecter of our faith, who for the joy that was set before Him, endured the cross, disregarding the shame, and has now taken His seat at the right hand of the throne of God.

Jude 24-25

וְהוּא אֲשֶׁר יָכוֹל לִשְׁמֹר אֶתְכֶם מִמִּכְשׁוֹל וּלְהַעֲמִיד אֶתְכֶם
לִפְנֵי כְּבוֹדוֹ נְקִיִּים מִדֹּפִי וּמְלֵאֵי שִׂמְחָה, הָאֱלֹהִים הַיָּחִיד,
מוֹשִׁיעֵנוּ עַל־יְדֵי יֵשׁוּעַ הַמָּשִׁיחַ אֲדוֹנֵנוּ, לוֹ הַכָּבוֹד וְהַגְּדֻלָּה
וְהָעֹז וְהַשִּׁלְטוֹן לִפְנֵי כָּל עוֹלָם, גַּם עַתָּה גַּם לְכָל הָעוֹלָמִים.
אָמֵן.

Now to the One who is able to guard you from stumbling, and to cause you to stand with great joy before the presence of His glory without blemish, to the only God our Saviour, through Messiah Yeshua our Lord, be glory, majesty, sovereignty and power, before all time, and now, and for all eternity. Amen.

(Conclude with a reflection on the soon return of Messiah Yeshua and the establishment of His earthly Kingdom)

Birkat HaMazon

(On weekdays recite Psalm 137)

עַל נַהֲרוֹת בָּבֶל שָׁם יָשַׁבְנוּ גַּם בָּכִינוּ בְּזָכְרֵנוּ אֶת צִיּוֹן. עַל עֲרָבִים בְּתוֹכָהּ תָּלִינוּ כִּנּוֹרוֹתֵינוּ. כִּי שָׁם שְׁאֵלוּנוּ שׁוֹבֵינוּ דִּבְרֵי שִׁיר, וְתוֹלָלֵינוּ שִׂמְחָה; שִׁירוּ לָנוּ מִשִּׁיר צִיּוֹן. אֵיךְ נָשִׁיר אֶת שִׁיר יְיָ עַל אַדְמַת נֵכָר. אִם אֶשְׁכָּחֵךְ יְרוּשָׁלָיִם, תִּשְׁכַּח יְמִינִי. תִּדְבַּק לְשׁוֹנִי לְחִכִּי, אִם לֹא אֶזְכְּרֵכִי, אִם לֹא אַעֲלֶה אֶת יְרוּשָׁלַיִם עַל רֹאשׁ שִׂמְחָתִי. זְכֹר יְיָ לִבְנֵי אֱדוֹם אֵת יוֹם יְרוּשָׁלָיִם; הָאֹמְרִים עָרוּ עָרוּ, עַד הַיְסוֹד בָּהּ. בַּת בָּבֶל הַשְּׁדוּדָה, אַשְׁרֵי שֶׁיְשַׁלֶּם לָךְ אֶת גְּמוּלֵךְ שֶׁגָּמַלְתְּ לָנוּ. אַשְׁרֵי שֶׁיֹּאחֵז וְנִפֵּץ אֶת עֹלָלַיִךְ אֶל הַסָּלַע.

By the waters of Babylon, there we sat down and wept, when we remembered Tsiyon. On the willows there we hung up our harps. For there our captors required of us songs, and our tormentors, laughter, saying, "Sing us one of the songs of Tsiyon!" How can we sing the Lord's song in a foreign land? If I forget you, O Jerusalem, let my right hand shrivel up! Let my tongue stick to the roof of my mouth, if I do not remember you, if I do not set Jerusalem above my highest joy! Remember, O Lord, against the Edomites the day of Jerusalem, how they said, "Destroy it, destroy it! Down to its foundations!" O daughter of Babylon, you devastator! Happy will be the one who repays you with what you have done to us! Happy will be the one who takes your little ones and dashes them against the rock!

(On Shabbat, Yom Tov & Rosh Ḥodesh recite Psalm 126)

שִׁיר הַמַּעֲלוֹת. בְּשׁוּב יְיָ אֶת שִׁיבַת צִיּוֹן הָיִינוּ כְּחֹלְמִים. אָז יִמָּלֵא שְׂחוֹק פִּינוּ, וּלְשׁוֹנֵנוּ רִנָּה; אָז יֹאמְרוּ בַגּוֹיִם, הִגְדִּיל יְיָ לַעֲשׂוֹת עִם אֵלֶּה. הִגְדִּיל יְיָ לַעֲשׂוֹת עִמָּנוּ, הָיִינוּ שְׂמֵחִים. שׁוּבָה יְיָ אֶת שְׁבִיתֵנוּ, כַּאֲפִיקִים בַּנֶּגֶב. הַזֹּרְעִים בְּדִמְעָה, בְּרִנָּה יִקְצֹרוּ. הָלוֹךְ יֵלֵךְ וּבָכֹה נֹשֵׂא מֶשֶׁךְ הַזָּרַע; בֹּא יָבוֹא בְרִנָּה נֹשֵׂא אֲלֻמֹּתָיו.

Shir Hama'alot, b'shuv Adonai et shivat Tsiyon hayinu k'ḥol'mim. Az yimalei s'ḥok pinu ul'shoneinu rinah. Az yom'ru vagoyim higdil Adonai la̅'asot im eileh. Higdil Adonai la'asot imanu hayinu s'meiḥim. Shuvah Adonai et sheviteinu, ka'afikim banegev. Hazor'im b'dimah, b'rinah yik'tsoru. Halokh Yeileikh uvakhoh noseih meshekh haza'ra, bo yavo v'rinah nosei alumotayv.

When the Lord restored the fortunes of Tsiyon, we were like those who dream. Then our mouth was filled with laughter, and our tongue with shouts of joy; then they said among the nations, "The Lord has done great things for them." The Lord has done great things for us; we are glad. Restore our fortunes, O Lord, like the streams in the Negeb! May those who sow in tears reap with shouts of joy! He that goes forth weeping, bearing the seed for sowing, shall come home with shouts of joy, bringing his sheaves with him.

(Recite the zimmun if three or more have eaten together; include words in parentheses when a minyan is present. Wedding zimmun is on page 49)

(The Leader selected by the group begins the zimmun)

Ḥaveiray n'vareikh! חֲבֵרַי נְבָרֵךְ.

Friends, let us give blessing!

(Those around the table respond)

יְהִי שֵׁם יְיָ מְבֹרָךְ מֵעַתָּה וְעַד עוֹלָם.

Y'hi sheim Adonai m'vorakh mei-atah v'ad olam.
May the Name of the Lord be blessed both now and forever!

(The Leader says)

יְהִי שֵׁם יְיָ מְבֹרָךְ מֵעַתָּה וְעַד עוֹלָם.
בִּרְשׁוּת חֲבֵרַי, נְבָרֵךְ (אֱלֹהֵינוּ) שֶׁאָכַלְנוּ מִשֶּׁלּוֹ.

Y'hi sheim Adonai m'vorakh mei-atah v'ad olam.
Birshut ḥaveiray, n'vareikh (Eloheinu) she-akha-lenu mishelo.

May the Name of the Lord be blessed both now and forever!
With your permission Friends, let us shout with joy, (blessing God) for the bounty we have shared.

(Those around the table respond and then the Leader repeats)

בָּרוּךְ (אֱלֹהֵינוּ) שֶׁאָכַלְנוּ מִשֶּׁלּוֹ וּבְטוּבוֹ חָיִינוּ.

Barukh (Eloheinu) she-akha-lenu mishelo uv'tuvo ḥayinu.

Blessed (is our God), for the bounty we have shared, and whose goodness is upon our life.

(Together)

Barukh hu uvarukh sh'mo בָּרוּךְ הוּא וּבָרוּךְ שְׁמוֹ.

Blessed is He and blessed is His Name!

בָּרוּךְ אַתָּה יְיָ, אֱלֹהֵינוּ מֶלֶךְ הָעוֹלָם, הַזָּן אֶת הָעוֹלָם כֻּלּוֹ בְּטוּבוֹ בְּחֵן בְּחֶסֶד וּבְרַחֲמִים. הוּא נוֹתֵן לֶחֶם לְכָל בָּשָׂר כִּי לְעוֹלָם חַסְדּוֹ. וּבְטוּבוֹ הַגָּדוֹל תָּמִיד לֹא חָסַר לָנוּ, וְאַל יֶחְסַר לָנוּ מָזוֹן לְעוֹלָם וָעֶד, בַּעֲבוּר שְׁמוֹ הַגָּדוֹל. כִּי הוּא אֵל זָן וּמְפַרְנֵס לַכֹּל וּמֵטִיב לַכֹּל. וּמֵכִין מָזוֹן לְכָל בְּרִיּוֹתָיו אֲשֶׁר בָּרָא. בָּרוּךְ אַתָּה יְיָ, הַזָּן אֶת הַכֹּל.

Barukh atah Adonai, Eloheinu Melekh haolam, hazan et ha-olam kulo b'tuvo, b'ḥein b'ḥesed uv'raḥamim. Hu notein leḥem l'khol basar ki l'olam ḥasdo. Uv'tuvo hagadol tamid lo ḥasar lanu, v'al yeḥsar lanu, mazon l'olam va-ed, baavur sh'mo hagadol. Ki hu Eil zan um'farneis lakol umeitiv lakol, umeikhin mazon l'khol b'riyotav asher bara. Barukh atah Adonai, hazan et hakol.

Blessed are You, Lord our God, King of the Universe, who, through His goodness, nourishes the whole world with grace, loving kindness and compassion. Indeed, "He gives bread to all flesh because His loving kindness endures forever." His great goodness, with which we are sustained, has never diminished toward us; nor will it ever, for the sake of His great Name. He is God who provides nourishment for all, and who does good to all. He provides food for all His creation. Blessed are You, Lord, who provides food for all.

(An Abridged Version can be followed from here on page 44. A very brief version of Birkat HaMazon that contains just the traditional minimal requirements to mention the Food, the Land of Israel, Jerusalem's sanctity and God's Goodness after eating can be found on page 75)

נוֹדֶה לְּךָ יְיָ אֱלֹהֵינוּ עַל שֶׁהִנְחַלְתָּ לַאֲבוֹתֵינוּ, אֶרֶץ חֶמְדָּה
טוֹבָה וּרְחָבָה. וְעַל שֶׁהוֹצֵאתָנוּ יְיָ אֱלֹהֵינוּ מֵאֶרֶץ מִצְרַיִם,
וּפְדִיתָנוּ, מִבֵּית עֲבָדִים. וְעַל בְּרִיתְךָ שֶׁחָתַמְתָּ בִּבְשָׂרֵנוּ.
וְעַל תּוֹרָתְךָ שֶׁלִּמַּדְתָּנוּ. וְעַל חֻקֶּיךָ שֶׁהוֹדַעְתָּנוּ וְעַל חַיִּים חֵן
וָחֶסֶד שֶׁחוֹנַנְתָּנוּ. וְעַל אֲכִילַת מָזוֹן שָׁאַתָּה זָן וּמְפַרְנֵס
אוֹתָנוּ תָּמִיד, בְּכָל יוֹם וּבְכָל עֵת וּבְכָל שָׁעָה.

Nodeh l'kha, Adonai Eloheinu, al shehin'ḥa'leta la'avoteinu, erets ḥemdah tovah ur'ḥavah. V'al shehotseitanu Adonai Eloheinu mei-erets Mitsrayim, uf'ditanu, mibeit avadim. V'al b'rit'kha sheḥata'meta biv'sareinu. V'al Torat'kha sheli'madtanu. V'al ḥukekha shehoda'tanu v'al ḥayim ḥein vaḥesed sheḥonan'tanu. V'al akhilat mazon sha'atah zan um'farneis otanu tamid, b'khol yom uv'khol eit uv'khol sha'ah.

Lord our God, we thank You that besides this, You have given as an inheritance to our fathers a desirable, good, and abundant land. And besides this, Lord our God, You have brought us out of the land of Egypt, ransoming us from the house of slavery. And besides this, You have given us the sign of the covenant upon our flesh. And besides this, You have given us Your instruction that we might study. And besides this, You have made Your precepts known to us. And besides this, You have pardoned us, giving us a life of grace and loving kindness. And besides this, You have given us food to eat; food which nourishes us always: every day, and every season, and every hour.

(On Ḥanukah, Purim and Yom Ha'atsmaut say)

עַל הַנִּסִּים וְעַל הַפֻּרְקָן, וְעַל הַגְּבוּרוֹת, וְעַל הַתְּשׁוּעוֹת וְעַל
הַמִּלְחָמוֹת שֶׁעָשִׂיתָ לַאֲבוֹתֵינוּ בַּיָּמִים הָהֵם בַּזְּמַן הַזֶּה.

Al hanisim v'al hapurkan, v'al hag'vurot, v'al hat'shu-ot, v'al hamil'ḥamot sheh-asitah la'avoteinu bayameem haheim baz'man hazeh.

We thank you for the miracles, for the redemption, for the mighty deeds, for the saving acts, and for the battles which You have done for our ancestors in those days, at this time.

(On Ḥanukah add)

בִּימֵי מַתִּתְיָהוּ בֶּן יוֹחָנָן כֹּהֵן גָּדוֹל, חַשְׁמוֹנַאי וּבָנָיו, כְּשֶׁעָמְדָה
מַלְכוּת יָוָן הָרְשָׁעָה עַל עַמְּךָ יִשְׂרָאֵל לְהַשְׁכִּיחָם תּוֹרָתֶךָ,
וּלְהַעֲבִירָם מֵחֻקֵּי רְצוֹנֶךָ, וְאַתָּה בְּרַחֲמֶיךָ הָרַבִּים עָמַדְתָּ לָהֶם
בְּעֵת צָרָתָם, רַבְתָּ אֶת רִיבָם, דַּנְתָּ אֶת דִּינָם, נָקַמְתָּ אֶת
נִקְמָתָם, מָסַרְתָּ גִּבּוֹרִים בְּיַד חַלָּשִׁים, וְרַבִּים בְּיַד מְעַטִּים,
וּטְמֵאִים בְּיַד טְהוֹרִים, וּרְשָׁעִים בְּיַד צַדִּיקִים, וְזֵדִים בְּיַד
עוֹסְקֵי תוֹרָתֶךָ. וּלְךָ עָשִׂיתָ שֵׁם גָּדוֹל וְקָדוֹשׁ בְּעוֹלָמֶךָ, וּלְעַמְּךָ
יִשְׂרָאֵל עָשִׂיתָ תְּשׁוּעָה גְדוֹלָה וּפֻרְקָן כְּהַיּוֹם הַזֶּה. וְאַחַר כֵּן
בָּאוּ בָנֶיךָ לִדְבִיר בֵּיתֶךָ, וּפִנּוּ אֶת הֵיכָלֶךָ, וְטִהֲרוּ אֶת
מִקְדָּשֶׁךָ, וְהִדְלִיקוּ נֵרוֹת בְּחַצְרוֹת קָדְשֶׁךָ, וְקָבְעוּ שְׁמוֹנַת יְמֵי
חֲנֻכָּה אֵלּוּ, לְהוֹדוֹת וּלְהַלֵּל לְשִׁמְךָ הַגָּדוֹל, וּבְעֵת רְצוֹנְךָ
שָׁלַחְתָּ לָנוּ אֶת־יֵשׁוּעַ מְשִׁיחֵנוּ, אוֹר הָעוֹלָם.

In the days of the Hasmonean Matityahu son of Yoḥanan the High Priest, and his sons, when stood the wicked kingdom of the Hellenists against Your people Israel to cause them to abandon Your Torah and to turn from the statutes of your will, You in Your great compassion stood for them in their time of tribulation. You contended for them in their fight, judged for them in their judgment, avenged them in their vengeance, and delivered them by means of heroes when they were weak; the many into the hands of the few, the unclean into the hands of the clean, the wicked into the hands of the righteous, and the deceiver into the hands of those who practiced Your Torah. Your great and holy Name is established in Your world, and You have established a great salvation for Your people Israel, and have redeemed them from that day to this. Indeed, after this Your children came into the holy place of Your house, we cleared Your Temple of defilement, and purified Your holy sanctuary, and lit the lights in Your holy court, and established the lighting of the lights in the eight days of Ḥanukah, to thank and to praise the greatness of Your Name, and at the time pleasing to you, sent Yeshua, our Messiah, the Light of the World.

(On Purim add)

בִּימֵי מָרְדְּכַי וְאֶסְתֵּר בְּשׁוּשַׁן הַבִּירָה, כְּשֶׁעָמַד עֲלֵיהֶם הָמָן הָרָשָׁע, בִּקֵּשׁ לְהַשְׁמִיד לַהֲרֹג וּלְאַבֵּד אֶת כָּל הַיְּהוּדִים, מִנַּעַר וְעַד זָקֵן, טַף וְנָשִׁים, בְּיוֹם אֶחָד, בִּשְׁלוֹשָׁה עָשָׂר לְחֹדֶשׁ שְׁנֵים עָשָׂר, הוּא חֹדֶשׁ אֲדָר, וּשְׁלָלָם לָבוֹז. וְאַתָּה בְּרַחֲמֶיךָ הָרַבִּים הֵפַרְתָּ אֶת עֲצָתוֹ, וְקִלְקַלְתָּ אֶת מַחֲשַׁבְתּוֹ, וַהֲשֵׁבוֹתָ לּוֹ גְּמוּלוֹ בְּרֹאשׁוֹ, וְתָלוּ אוֹתוֹ וְאֶת בָּנָיו עַל הָעֵץ.

In the days of Mordecai and Esther, in the capital city of Shushan, when the wicked Haman stood against them, asking that all the Jews be annihilated, murdered, and destroyed, both young and old, infants and women, and to take their plunder, in one day, on the thirteenth day of the twelfth month, which is Adar. You, in Your great compassion, annulled this decree, spoiling his purposes, and returning to him judgement upon his own head, that both he and his sons would hang upon the tree.

(On other days continue here)

וְעַל הַכֹּל יְיָ אֱלֹהֵינוּ אֲנַחְנוּ מוֹדִים לָךְ, וּמְבָרְכִים אוֹתָךְ. יִתְבָּרַךְ שִׁמְךָ בְּפִי כָּל חַי תָּמִיד לְעוֹלָם וָעֶד. כַּכָּתוּב, וְאָכַלְתָּ וְשָׂבָעְתָּ, וּבֵרַכְתָּ אֶת יְיָ אֱלֹהֶיךָ עַל הָאָרֶץ הַטֹּבָה אֲשֶׁר נָתַן לָךְ. בָּרוּךְ אַתָּה יְיָ, עַל הָאָרֶץ וְעַל הַמָּזוֹן.

V'al hakol, Adonai Eloheinu, anaḥnu modim lakh, u'mevar'khim otakh. Yit'barakh shim'ka b'fi kol ḥai tamid l'olam va-ed. Kakatuv, v'akhal'ta v'sava'ta, uveirakhta et Adonai Elohekha al ha'arets hatovah asher natan lakh. Barukh atah Adonai, al ha'arets v'al hamazon.

And besides all these things, Lord our God, we give You thanks and bless You for Your miracles. Your Name will be magnified by the mouth of all who live, forever and to all eternity. As it is written, "You shall eat and be satisfied, and give blessing to the Lord your God for the good land He has given to you." Blessed are You, Lord, for the land and for its produce.

רַחֵם יְיָ אֱלֹהֵינוּ, עַל יִשְׂרָאֵל עַמֶּךָ, וְעַל יְרוּשָׁלַיִם עִירֶךָ, וְעַל צִיּוֹן מִשְׁכַּן כְּבוֹדֶךָ, וְעַל מַלְכוּת בֵּית דָּוִד מְשִׁיחֶךָ, וְעַל הַבַּיִת הַגָּדוֹל וְהַקָּדוֹשׁ שֶׁנִּקְרָא שִׁמְךָ עָלָיו. אֱלֹהֵינוּ, אָבִינוּ, רְעֵנוּ, זוּנֵנוּ, פַּרְנְסֵנוּ, וְכַלְכְּלֵנוּ, וְהַרְוִיחֵנוּ, וְהַרְוַח לָנוּ יְיָ אֱלֹהֵינוּ מְהֵרָה מִכָּל צָרוֹתֵינוּ, וְנָא, אַל תַּצְרִיכֵנוּ. יְיָ אֱלֹהֵינוּ, לֹא לִידֵי מַתְּנַת בָּשָׂר וָדָם, וְלֹא לִידֵי הַלְוָאָתָם. כִּי אִם לְיָדְךָ הַמְּלֵאָה, הַפְּתוּחָה, הַקְּדוֹשָׁה וְהָרְחָבָה. שֶׁלֹּא נֵבוֹשׁ וְלֹא נִכָּלֵם לְעוֹלָם וָעֶד.

Raḥeim, Adonai Eloheinu, al Yisraeil amekha, v'al Y'rushalayim ireka, v'al Tsiyon mishkan k'vodeka, v'al malkhut beit David M'shiḥeka. V'al habayit hagadol v'hakadosh shenikra shimka alayv. Eloheinu Avinu, r'einu zuneinu, par'neseinu v'khal'keleinu v'harviḥeinu, v'har'vaḥ lanu, Adonai Eloheinu, m'heirah mikol tsaro'teinu, v'na al tats'ri-kheinu, Adonai Eloheinu, lo lidei mat'nat basar vadam, v'lo lidei hal'va-atam, ki im l'yad'kha ham'lei-ah, hap'tuḥah hak'doshah v'har'ḥavah. Shelo neivosh v'lo nikaleim l'olam va-ed.

Lord our God, in time, have compassion upon Israel Your people, and upon Jerusalem Your city, and upon Tsiyon the dwelling place of Your glory, and upon the kingdom of the House of David Your Anointed, and upon the great and holy House on which Your Name has been named. Our God, our Father, our Shepherd, our Sustainer, our Supporter, and our Provider, provide for us, Lord our God, bringing relief from all our present troubles. Lord our God, may we never depend on gifts or loans from the hand of flesh and blood, but only from Your hand: overflowing, open, holy, and bountiful. May we never be shamed by others nor ashamed of ourselves.

(On Shabbat add)

רְצֵה וְהַחֲלִיצֵנוּ יְיָ אֱלֹהֵינוּ בְּמִצְוֹתֶיךָ וּבְמִצְוַת יוֹם הַשְּׁבִיעִי הַשַּׁבָּת הַגָּדוֹל וְהַקָּדוֹשׁ הַזֶּה. כִּי יוֹם זֶה גָּדוֹל וְקָדוֹשׁ הוּא לְפָנֶיךָ. לִשְׁבָּת בּוֹ וְלָנוּחַ בּוֹ בְּאַהֲבָה כְּמִצְוַת רְצוֹנֶךָ וּבִרְצוֹנְךָ הָנִיחַ לָנוּ יְיָ אֱלֹהֵינוּ, שֶׁלֹּא תְהֵא צָרָה וְיָגוֹן וַאֲנָחָה בְּיוֹם מְנוּחָתֵנוּ. וְהַרְאֵנוּ יְיָ אֱלֹהֵינוּ בְּנֶחָמַת צִיּוֹן עִירֶךָ, וּבְבִנְיַן יְרוּשָׁלַיִם עִיר קָדְשֶׁךָ, כִּי אַתָּה הוּא בַּעַל הַיְשׁוּעוֹת וּבַעַל הַנֶּחָמוֹת.

R'tsei v'haḥalitsei'nu Adonai Eloheinu b'mitsvotekha uv'mitsvat yom hash'vi'i hashabbat hagadol v'hakadosh hazeh. Ki yom zeh gadol v'kadosh hu l'fane-kha. Lish'bat bo v'lanuaḥ bo b'ahavah k'mitsvat r'tsonekha uvir'tson'kha hani'aḥ lanu Adonai Eloheinu, shelo t'hei tsarah v'yagon va'anaḥeh b'yom m'nuḥateinu. V'har'ei'nu Adonai Eloheinu b'neḥamat Tsiyon irekha, uv'vinyan Y'rushalayim ir kad'shekha, ki atah hu ba'al hay'shuot uva'al haneḥamot.

Lord our God, may You take pleasure in strengthening us through all Your commandments and in the command concerning the seventh day, this great and holy Shabbat. For before Your countenance, this day is great and holy; that we might dwell in Your rest and in Your love, in keeping with the desire of Your command. And may it be Your will, Lord our God, to grant us such rest; that there be no misfortune, or grief, or sighing on the day of our rest. Lord our God, may we behold Tsiyon Your city being comforted, and our descendents in Jerusalem Your holy city, for You are the Master of all salvation, and the Master of all consolation.

(On Rosh Ḥodesh and Festivals add)

אֱלֹהֵינוּ וֵאלֹהֵי אֲבוֹתֵינוּ, יַעֲלֶה וְיָבֹא וְיַגִּיעַ, וְיֵרָאֶה, וְיֵרָצֶה, וְיִשָּׁמַע, וְיִפָּקֵד, וְיִזָּכֵר זִכְרוֹנֵנוּ וּפִקְדוֹנֵנוּ, וְזִכְרוֹן אֲבוֹתֵינוּ, וְזִכְרוֹן מָשִׁיחַ יֵשׁוּעַ בֶּן דָּוִד עַבְדֶּךָ, וְזִכְרוֹן יְרוּשָׁלַיִם עִיר קָדְשֶׁךָ, וְזִכְרוֹן כָּל עַמְּךָ בֵּית יִשְׂרָאֵל לְפָנֶיךָ, לִפְלֵיטָה לְטוֹבָה לְחֵן וּלְחֶסֶד וּלְרַחֲמִים, לְחַיִּים וּלְשָׁלוֹם בְּיוֹם

Eloheinu ve-Elohei Avoteinu, ya'aleh ve-yavo ve-yagi'a, ve-yeira'eh, ve-yeiratseh, ve-yishama, ve-yipakeid, ve-yizakheir zikh'roneinu u-fik'doneinu, ve-zikh'ron avoteinu, ve-zikh'ron Mashi'aḥ Yeishua ben David av'dekha, ve-zikh'ron Yerushalayim ir kod'shekha, ve-zikh'ron kol am'kha beit Yisra'el lefanekha, li-f'leitah le-tovah, le- ḥein u-le-ḥesed u-le-raḥamim, le-ḥayim u-le-shalom, be-yom ...

Our God, and God of our fathers, may the remembrance and the consideration of us, and the remembrance of our fathers, and the remembrance of Messiah Yeshua, the son of David Your servant, and the remembrance of Jerusalem Your holy city, and the remembrance of all Your people, the House of Israel, arise and come, and reach, and be seen, and be accepted, and be heard, and be numbered, and be remembered before Your face; for deliverance, for favor, for grace and for loving kindness, and for compassion, and for peace on this day of ...

לְרֹאשׁ הַחֹדֶשׁ: רֹאשׁ הַחֹדֶשׁ

On Rosh Ḥodesh say: *Rosh HaḤodesh* (the New Month)

לְפֶסַח: חַג הַמַּצּוֹת

On Pesaḥ say: *Ḥag HaMatsot* (the Festival of Unleavened Bread)

לְשָׁבֻעוֹת: חַג הַשָּׁבֻעוֹת

On Shavuot say: *Ḥag HaShavuot* (the Festival of Weeks)

לְרֹאשׁ הַשָּׁנָה: הַזִּכָּרוֹן

On Rosh Hashanah say: *HaZikaron* (the Rememberance)

לְסֻכּוֹת: חַג הַסֻּכּוֹת

On Sukkot say: *Ḥag HaSukkot* (the Festival of Tabernacles)

לִשְׁמִינִי עֲצֶרֶת: הַשְּׁמִינִי חַג הָעֲצֶרֶת

On Shemini Atseret say: *HaShemini Ḥag Ha'atseret* (the Festival of the Eighth Day)

... הַזֶּה. זָכְרֵנוּ יְיָ אֱלֹהֵינוּ בּוֹ לְטוֹבָה. וּפָקְדֵנוּ בוֹ לִבְרָכָה, וְהוֹשִׁיעֵנוּ בוֹ לְחַיִּים. וּבִדְבַר יְשׁוּעָה וְרַחֲמִים, חוּס וְחָנֵּנוּ, וְרַחֵם עָלֵינוּ וְהוֹשִׁיעֵנוּ. כִּי אֵלֶיךָ עֵינֵינוּ, כִּי אֵל מֶלֶךְ חַנּוּן וְרַחוּם אָתָּה.

... ha-zeh. Zokh'reinu, Adonai Eloheinu, boh le-tovah. U-fokdeinu voh li-v'rakhah, ve-hoshi'einu voh le-ḥayim. U-vid'var yeishuah ve-raḥamim, ḥus ve-ḥaneinu, ve-raheim aleinu ve-hoshi'einu. Ki eilekha eineinu, ki El Melekh ḥanun ve-raḥum atah.

... Lord our God, remember us for goodness. Command blessing for us, and save us that we might live. Concerning salvation and compassion, take pity and pardon us, and have compassion on us, for You are our salvation. Our eyes are lifted to You, for You, God, are a gracious and compassionate King.

(On other days continue here)

וּבְנֵה יְרוּשָׁלַיִם עִיר הַקֹּדֶשׁ בִּמְהֵרָה בְיָמֵינוּ. בָּרוּךְ אַתָּה יְיָ, בּוֹנֵה בְרַחֲמָיו יְרוּשָׁלָיִם. אָמֵן.

Uv'neih Y'rushalayim ir hakodesh bimheirah v'yameinu. Barukh atah Adonai, boneih v'raḥamav Y'rushalayim. Amein.

Rebuild Jerusalem as a holy city very soon, even in our day. Blessed are You, Lord, who, in compassion, builds Jerusalem. Amen.

בָּרוּךְ אַתָּה יְיָ אֱלֹהֵינוּ מֶלֶךְ הָעוֹלָם, הָאֵל אָבִינוּ, מַלְכֵּנוּ, אַדִּירֵנוּ בּוֹרְאֵנוּ, גּוֹאֲלֵנוּ, יוֹצְרֵנוּ, קְדוֹשֵׁנוּ קְדוֹשׁ יַעֲקֹב, רוֹעֵנוּ רוֹעֵה יִשְׂרָאֵל. הַמֶּלֶךְ הַטּוֹב וְהַמֵּטִיב לַכֹּל. שֶׁבְּכָל יוֹם וָיוֹם הוּא הֵטִיב, הוּא מֵטִיב, הוּא יֵיטִיב לָנוּ. הוּא גְמָלָנוּ, הוּא גוֹמְלֵנוּ, הוּא יִגְמְלֵנוּ לָעַד לְחֵן וּלְחֶסֶד וּלְרַחֲמִים וּלְרֶוַח הַצָּלָה וְהַצְלָחָה בְּרָכָה וִישׁוּעָה, נֶחָמָה, פַּרְנָסָה וְכַלְכָּלָה, וְרַחֲמִים, וְחַיִּים וְשָׁלוֹם, וְכָל טוֹב. וּמִכָּל טוּב לְעוֹלָם אַל יְחַסְּרֵנוּ.

Barukh atah Adonai, Eloheinu Melekh Ha'Olam, ha-El Avinu Malkeinu Adireinu, Bor'einu, Goaleinu, Yots'reinu, K'dosheinu, K'dosh Yaakov, Ro-einu Ro-eih Yisraeil, HaMelekh hatov v'hameitiv lakol, sheb'khol yom vayom hu heitiv, hu meitiv, hu yeitiv lanu. Hu g'malanu, hu gom'leinu, hu yigm'leinu la'ad, l'ḥein ul'ḥesed ul'raḥamim ul'revaḥ, hatsalah v'hatslaḥah, b'rakhah vishuah, neḥamah, parnasah, v'khalkalah, v'raḥamim v'ḥayim v'shalom, v'khol tov. Umikol tov l'olam al y'ḥas'reinu.

Blessed are You, Lord our God, King of the Universe, God our Father, our King, our Mighty One, our Creator, our Redeemer, our Maker, our Holy One and the Holy One of Jacob, our Shepherd and the Shepherd of Israel. The Good King is good to all. Each day and every day, He has done good. He has done good, and He continually does good for us. He has dealt bountifully with us, He deals bountifully with us, and He will always deal bountifully with us; for grace, and for loving kindness, and for compassion, and for the wind of relief and success, blessing and deliverance, comfort, sustenance and support, and mercy, and life and peace, and with all that is good. May God, who knows our need, always provide us with good.

הָרַחֲמָן, הוּא יִמְלוֹךְ עָלֵינוּ לְעוֹלָם וָעֶד.

The Compassionate One, may He rule over us forever and ever.

הָרַחֲמָן, הוּא יִתְבָּרַךְ בַּשָּׁמַיִם וּבָאָרֶץ.

The Compassionate One, may He be blessed in the heavens and in the earth.

הָרַחֲמָן, הוּא יִשְׁתַּבַּח לְדוֹר דּוֹרִים, וְיִתְפָּאַר בָּנוּ לָעַד וּלְנֵצַח נְצָחִים, וְיִתְהַדַּר בָּנוּ לָעַד וּלְעוֹלְמֵי עוֹלָמִים.

The Compassionate One, may He be praised in all generations, and glorified in us forever and to all eternity, and honored among us forever, both in this world and in all worlds to come.

הָרַחֲמָן, הוּא יְפַרְנְסֵנוּ בְּכָבוֹד.

The Compassionate One, may He satisfy us with honor.

הָרַחֲמָן, הוּא יִשְׁבּוֹר עֻלֵּנוּ מֵעַל צַוָּארֵנוּ וְהוּא יוֹלִיכֵנוּ קוֹמְמִיּוּת לְאַרְצֵנוּ.

The Compassionate One, may He remove the yoke from our neck, that we might walk upright to our land.

הָרַחֲמָן, הוּא יִשְׁלַח בְּרָכָה מְרֻבָּה בַּבַּיִת הַזֶּה, וְעַל שֻׁלְחָן זֶה שֶׁאָכַלְנוּ עָלָיו.

The Compassionate One, may He multiply blessings upon us and upon this house, upon this table at which we have eaten.

הָרַחֲמָן, הוּא יִשְׁלַח לָנוּ אֶת אֵלִיָּהוּ הַנָּבִיא זָכוּר לַטּוֹב, וִיבַשֶּׂר לָנוּ בְּשׂוֹרוֹת טוֹבוֹת יְשׁוּעוֹת וְנֶחָמוֹת.

The Compassionate One, may He send us Elijah the Prophet, of good memory, bearing good tidings of salvation and consolation.

(When eating in one's own home)

הָרַחֲמָן הוּא יְבָרֵךְ אֶת אָבִי מוֹרִי בַּעַל הַבַּיִת הַזֶּה, וְאֶת אִמִּי מוֹרָתִי בַּעֲלַת הַבַּיִת הַזֶּה.

The Compassionate One, may He bless my honored father, the master of this house, and my honored mother, the mistress of this house.

(Blessing recited by a guest for the one hosting the meal)

הָרַחֲמָן, הוּא יְבָרֵךְ אֶת־(אָבִי מוֹרִי,) בַּעַל הַבַּיִת הַזֶּה,
וְאֶת־(אִמִּי מוֹרָתִי,) בַּעֲלַת הַבַּיִת הַזֶּה, אוֹתָם וְאֶת־בֵּיתָם
וְאֶת־זַרְעָם וְאֶת־כָּל אֲשֶׁר לָהֶם. אוֹתָנוּ וְאֶת כָּל אֲשֶׁר
לָנוּ, כְּמוֹ שֶׁנִּתְבָּרְכוּ אֲבוֹתֵינוּ, אַבְרָהָם יִצְחָק וְיַעֲקֹב. בַּכֹּל,
מִכֹּל, כֹּל. כֵּן יְבָרֵךְ אוֹתָנוּ כֻּלָּנוּ יַחַד. בִּבְרָכָה שְׁלֵמָה,
וְנֹאמַר אָמֵן.

The Compassionate One, may He bless (my father,) the master of this house, and (my mother,) the mistress of this house; and with them, this house, and their children, and all that belongs to them. Bless us as well, and all that is ours, even as our fathers Abraham, Isaac and Jacob were blessed in everything, by everything, and with everything, so may He bless all of us with perfect blessing, and let us say amen.

בַּמָּרוֹם יְלַמְּדוּ עֲלֵיהֶם וְעָלֵינוּ זְכוּת, שֶׁתְּהֵא לְמִשְׁמֶרֶת
שָׁלוֹם. וְנִשָּׂא בְרָכָה מֵאֵת יְיָ וּצְדָקָה מֵאֱלֹהֵי יִשְׁעֵנוּ, וְנִמְצָא
חֵן וְשֵׂכֶל טוֹב בְּעֵינֵי אֱלֹהִים וְאָדָם.

May He who is on high remember, so that enduring peace may be upon them and upon all of us. Then we will receive blessing from the Lord, and justice from the God of our salvation, and we shall find grace and good understanding in the eyes of God and of man.

(On Shabbat say)

הָרַחֲמָן, הוּא יַנְחִילֵנוּ יוֹם שֶׁכֻּלּוֹ שַׁבָּת וּמְנוּחָה לְחַיֵּי
הָעוֹלָמִים.

Haraḥaman, hu yan'ḥileinu yom she-kulo Shabbat um'uḥah l'ḥayeiy ha-olamim.

The Compassionate One, may He cause us to come to that day which shall always be Shabbat, with rest in life everlasting.

(On Rosh Ḥodesh say)

הָרַחֲמָן, הוּא יְחַדֵּשׁ עָלֵינוּ אֶת הַחֹדֶשׁ הַזֶּה לְטוֹבָה וְלִבְרָכָה.

Haraḥaman, hu y'ḥadeish aleinu et haḥodesh hazeh l'tovah v'liv'rakhah.

The Compassionate One, may He renew this month to us, for goodness and for blessing.

(On a Yom Tov say)

הָרַחֲמָן, הוּא יַנְחִילֵנוּ יוֹם שֶׁכֻּלּוֹ טוֹב.

Haraḥaman, hu yan'ḥileinu yom shekulo tov.

The Compassionate One, may He cause us to come to that day that is always good.

(On Rosh Hashanah say)

הָרַחֲמָן, הוּא יְחַדֵּשׁ עָלֵינוּ אֶת הַשָּׁנָה הַזֹּאת לְטוֹבָה וְלִבְרָכָה.

Haraḥaman, hu y'ḥadeish aleinu et hashanah hazot l'tovah v'liv'rakhah.

The Compassionate One, may He renew this year for us, for good and for blessing.

(On Sukkot say)

הָרַחֲמָן, הוּא יָקִים לָנוּ אֶת סֻכַּת דָּוִד.

Haraḥaman, hu yakim lanu et Sukkat David.

The Compassionate One, may He raise up for us the Tabernacle of David.

(On other days continue here)

הָרַחֲמָן, הוּא יְבָרֵךְ אֶת־מְדִינַת יִשְׂרָאֵל, רֵאשִׁית צְמִיחַת גְּאֻלָּתֵנוּ.

Haraḥaman, hu y'vareikh et M'dinat Yisraeil, reisheet ts'miḥat g'oo-lateinu.

The Compassionate One, may He bless the State of Israel, the dawn of our redemption.

הָרַחֲמָן, הוּא יְבָרֵךְ אֶת־אַחֵינוּ בְּנֵי יִשְׂרָאֵל הַנְּתוּנִים בְּצָרָה, וְיוֹצִיאֵם מֵאֲפֵלָה לְאוֹרָה.

Haraḥaman, hu y'vareikh et aḥeinu b'nei Yisraeil ha'netunim b'tsarah, v'yotsi-eim mei-afeilah l'orah.

The Compassionate One, may He bless all of our people Israel who suffer, and bring them out of darkness into light.

הָרַחֲמָן, הוּא יְזַכֵּנוּ לִימוֹת הַמָּשִׁיחַ יֵשׁוּעַ וּלְחַיֵּי הָעוֹלָם הַבָּא.

Harahaman, hu y'zakeinu limot haMashiah Yeishua ul'hayeiy haolam haba.

The Compassionate One, may He declare us worthy of Messiah Yeshua and life in the world to come.

Magdil **מַגְדִּיל** *(On weekdays say)*

He makes great the ...

Migdol **מִגְדּוֹל** *(On Shabbat, Festivals and Rosh Hodesh say)*

He fortifies the ...

יְשׁוּעוֹת מַלְכּוֹ, וְעֹשֶׂה חֶסֶד לִמְשִׁיחוֹ לְדָוִד וּלְזַרְעוֹ עַד עוֹלָם. עֹשֶׂה שָׁלוֹם בִּמְרוֹמָיו, הוּא יַעֲשֶׂה שָׁלוֹם, עָלֵינוּ וְעַל כָּל יִשְׂרָאֵל, וְאִמְרוּ אָמֵן.

y'shuot malko, v'oseh hesed lim'shiho l'David ul'zaro ad olam. Oseh shalom bim'romayv, hu ya'aseh shalom, aleinu v'al kol Yisraeil, v'im'ru amein.

salvation of His Kingship, and shows loving kindness to His anointed, to David and to his seed forever. May He who creates peace in the high heavens, may He create peace for us, and for all Israel, and let us say amen.

יְראוּ אֶת יְיָ קְדֹשָׁיו, כִּי אֵין מַחְסוֹר לִירֵאָיו. כְּפִירִים רָשׁוּ וְרָעֵבוּ, וְדוֹרְשֵׁי יְיָ לֹא יַחְסְרוּ כָל טוֹב. הוֹדוּ לַייָ כִּי טוֹב, כִּי לְעוֹלָם חַסְדּוֹ. פּוֹתֵחַ אֶת יָדֶךָ, וּמַשְׂבִּיעַ לְכָל חַי רָצוֹן. בָּרוּךְ הַגֶּבֶר אֲשֶׁר יִבְטַח בַּייָ, וְהָיָה יְיָ מִבְטַחוֹ. נַעַר הָיִיתִי גַם זָקַנְתִּי וְלֹא רָאִיתִי צַדִּיק נֶעֱזָב, וְזַרְעוֹ מְבַקֶּשׁ לָחֶם. יְיָ עֹז לְעַמּוֹ יִתֵּן, יְיָ יְבָרֵךְ אֶת עַמּוֹ בַשָּׁלוֹם.

Fear the Lord, you, His holy ones, for there is no want to those who honor Him. Young lions may suffer want, but those who seek the Lord shall lack for no good thing. Give thanks to the Lord, for He is good; His loving kindness endures forever. You open Your hand and satisfy the desire of all who live. Blessed is the man whose trust is in the Lord, for the Lord will be his trust. I have been young, and now I am old, and I have never seen the righteous forsaken, and his seed having to beg for bread. The Lord will give strength to His people; the Lord will bless His people with peace.

Birkat HaMazon *(abridged version)*

נוֹדֶה לְּךָ יְיָ אֱלֹהֵינוּ עַל שֶׁהִנְחַלְתָּ לַאֲבוֹתֵינוּ, אֶרֶץ חֶמְדָּה טוֹבָה וּרְחָבָה. בְּרִית וְתוֹרָה, חַיִּים וּמָזוֹן. יִתְבָּרַךְ שִׁמְךָ בְּפִי כָּל חַי תָּמִיד לְעוֹלָם וָעֶד. כַּכָּתוּב, וְאָכַלְתָּ וְשָׂבָעְתָּ, וּבֵרַכְתָּ אֶת יְיָ אֱלֹהֶיךָ עַל הָאָרֶץ הַטֹּבָה אֲשֶׁר נָתַן לָךְ. בָּרוּךְ אַתָּה יְיָ, עַל הָאָרֶץ וְעַל הַמָּזוֹן.

Nodeh l'kha, Adonai Eloheinu, al shehin'ḥa'leta la'avoteinu, erets ḥemdah tovah u'reḥavah. B'rit v'Torah, ḥayim u'mazon. Yit'barakh shim'kha b'fi kol ḥai tamid l'olam va-ed. Kakatuv, v'akhal'ta v'sava'ta, u'veirakhta et Adonai Elohekha al ha'arets hatovah asher natan lakh. Barukh atah Adonai, al ha'arets v'al hamazon.

Lord our God, we thank You that besides this, You have given as an inheritance to our fathers a desirable, good, and abundant land; for the covenant and Torah, for life and food. Your Name will be magnified by the mouth of all who live, forever and to all eternity. As it is written, "You shall eat and be satisfied, and give blessing to the Lord your God for the good land He has given to you." Blessed are You, Lord, for the land and for its produce.

(On Ḥanukah, Purim and Yom Ha'atsmaut say)

עַל הַנִּסִּים וְעַל הַפֻּרְקָן, וְעַל הַגְּבוּרוֹת, וְעַל הַתְּשׁוּעוֹת וְעַל הַמִּלְחָמוֹת שֶׁעָשִׂיתָ לַאֲבוֹתֵינוּ בַּיָּמִים הָהֵם בַּזְּמַן הַזֶּה.

Al hanisim v'al hapurkan, v'al hag'vurot, v'al hat'shu-ot, v'al hamil'ḥamot sheh-asitah la'avoteinu bayameem haheim baz'man hazeh.

We thank you for the miracles, for the redemption, for the mighty deeds, for the saving acts, and for the battles which You have done for our ancestors in those days, at this time.

(Additionally, on Hanukah read page 33; on Purim read page 34)

(On other days continue here)

וּבְנֵה יְרוּשָׁלַיִם עִיר הַקֹּדֶשׁ בִּמְהֵרָה בְיָמֵינוּ. בָּרוּךְ אַתָּה יְיָ, בּוֹנֵה בְרַחֲמָיו יְרוּשָׁלָיִם. אָמֵן.

Uv'neih Y'rushalayim ir hakodesh bimheirah v'yameinu. Barukh atah Adonai, boneih v'raḥamayv Y'rushalayim. Amein.

Rebuild Jerusalem, the holy city very soon, even in our day. Blessed are You, Lord, who in compassion builds Jerusalem. Amen.

בָּרוּךְ אַתָּה יְיָ אֱלֹהֵינוּ מֶלֶךְ הָעוֹלָם, הַמֶּלֶךְ הַטּוֹב, וְהַמֵּטִיב לַכֹּל, הוּא הֵטִיב, הוּא מֵטִיב, הוּא יֵיטִיב לָנוּ. הוּא גְמָלָנוּ, הוּא גוֹמְלֵנוּ, הוּא יִגְמְלֵנוּ לָעַד לְחֵן וּלְחֶסֶד וּלְרַחֲמִים. וּמִכָּל טוּב לְעוֹלָם אַל יְחַסְּרֵנוּ.

Barukh atah Adonai Eloheinu Melekh Ha'Olam, HaMelekh hatov v'hameitiv lakol, hu heitiv, hu meitiv, hu yeitiv lanu. Hu g'malanu, hu gom'leinu, hu yigm'leinu la'ad l'ḥein ul'ḥesed ul'raḥamim, umikal tuv l'olam al y'ḥas'reinu.

Blessed are You, Lord our God, King of the Universe, the Good King who is good to all. He has done good, and He continually does good for us. He has dealt bountifully with us, He deals bountifully with us, and He will always deal bountifully with us; for grace, and for loving kindness, and for compassion. May God, who knows our need, always provide us with good.

(On Shabbat say)

הָרַחֲמָן, הוּא יַנְחִילֵנוּ יוֹם שֶׁכֻּלּוֹ שַׁבָּת וּמְנוּחָה לְחַיֵּי הָעוֹלָמִים.

Haraḥaman, hu yan'ḥileinu yom she-kulo Shabbat um'nuḥah l'ḥayeiy ha-olamim.

The Compassionate One, may He cause us to come to that day which shall always be Shabbat, with rest in life everlasting.

(On Rosh Ḥodesh say)

הָרַחֲמָן, הוּא יְחַדֵּשׁ עָלֵינוּ אֶת הַחֹדֶשׁ הַזֶּה לְטוֹבָה וְלִבְרָכָה.

Haraḥaman, hu y'ḥadeish aleinu et haḥodesh hazeh l'tovah v'liv'rakhah.

The Compassionate One, may He renew this month to us, for goodness and for blessing.

(On a Yom Tov say)

הָרַחֲמָן, הוּא יַנְחִילֵנוּ יוֹם שֶׁכֻּלּוֹ טוֹב.

Haraḥaman, hu yan'ḥileinu yom shekulo tov.

The Compassionate One, may He cause us to come to that day that is always good.

(On Rosh Hashanah say)

הָרַחֲמָן, הוּא יְחַדֵּשׁ עָלֵינוּ אֶת הַשָּׁנָה הַזֹּאת לְטוֹבָה וְלִבְרָכָה.

Haraḥaman, hu y'ḥadeish aleinu et hashanah hazot l'tovah v'liv'rakhah.

The Compassionate One, may He renew this year for us, for good and for blessing.

(On Sukkot say)

הָרַחֲמָן, הוּא יָקִים לָנוּ אֶת סֻכַּת דָּוִד.

Haraḥaman, hu yakim lanu et Sukkat David.

The Compassionate One, may He raise up for us the Tabernacle of David.

(On other days continue here)

הָרַחֲמָן, הוּא יְבָרֵךְ אֶת־מְדִינַת יִשְׂרָאֵל, רֵאשִׁית צְמִיחַת גְּאֻלָּתֵנוּ.

Haraḥaman, hu y'vareikh et M'dinat Yisraeil, reishit ts'miḥat g'u-lateinu.

The Compassionate One, may He bless the State of Israel, the dawn of our redemption.

הָרַחֲמָן, הוּא יְבָרֵךְ אֶת־אַחֵינוּ בְּנֵי יִשְׂרָאֵל הַנְּתוּנִים בְּצָרָה, וְיוֹצִיאֵם מֵאֲפֵלָה לְאוֹרָה.

Harahaman, hu y'vareikh et aheinu b'nei Yisraeil han'tunim b'tsarah, v'yotsi-eim mei-afeilah l'orah.

The Compassionate One, may He bless all of our people Israel who suffer, and bring them out of darkness into light.

הָרַחֲמָן, הוּא יְזַכֵּנוּ לִימוֹת הַמָּשִׁיחַ יֵשׁוּעַ וּלְחַיֵּי הָעוֹלָם הַבָּא.

Harahaman, hu y'zakeinu limot haMashiah Yeishua ul'hayeiy haolam haba.

The Compassionate One, may He declare us worthy of Messiah Yeshua and life in the world to come.

Magdil **מַגְדִּיל** *(On weekdays say)*

He makes great the ...

Migdol **מִגְדּוֹל** *(On Shabbat, Festivals and Rosh Hodesh say)*

He fortifies the ...

יְשׁוּעוֹת מַלְכּוֹ, וְעֹשֶׂה חֶסֶד לִמְשִׁיחוֹ לְדָוִד וּלְזַרְעוֹ עַד עוֹלָם. עֹשֶׂה שָׁלוֹם בִּמְרוֹמָיו, הוּא יַעֲשֶׂה שָׁלוֹם, עָלֵינוּ וְעַל כָּל יִשְׂרָאֵל, וְאִמְרוּ, אָמֵן.

y'shuot malko, v'oseh hesed lim'shiho l'David ul'zaro ad olam. Oseh shalom bim'romayv, hu ya'aseh shalom, aleinu v'al kal Yisraeil, v'im-ru amein.

salvation of His Kingship, and shows loving kindness to His anointed, to David and to his seed forever. May He who creates peace in the high heavens, may He create peace for us, and for all Israel, and let us say amen.

Birkat Blessings after a Wedding Meal

(This special Birkat zimmun begins after Shir Hamalot on page 29 after the wedding meal, and at any meal celebrating the wedding for the six days following the wedding . Two cups of wine and a third empty cup are needed. Begin here with the Leader holding the first cup of wine)

(The Leader selected by the group begins the zimmun)

Ḥaveiray n'vareikh! חֲבֵרַי נְבָרֵךְ.

Friends, let us give blessing!

(Those around the table respond and the Leader repeats)

יְהִי שֵׁם יְיָ מְבֹרָךְ מֵעַתָּה וְעַד עוֹלָם.

Y'hi sheim Adonai m'vorakh mei-atah v'ad olam.

May the Name of the Lord be blessed both now and forever!

(The Leader says)

דְּוַי הָסֵר וְגַם חָרוֹן, וְאָז אִלֵּם בְּשִׁיר יָרוֹן. נְחֵנוּ בְּמַעְגְּלֵי צֶדֶק. שְׁעֵה בִּרְכַּת בְּנֵי אַהֲרֹן. בִּרְשׁוּת חֲבֵרַי, נְבָרֵךְ אֱלֹהֵינוּ שֶׁהַשִּׂמְחָה בִּמְעוֹנוֹ וְשֶׁאָכַלְנוּ מִשֶּׁלּוֹ.

D'vay haseir v'gam ḥaron, v'az ileim b'shir yaron. N'ḥeinu b'ma-g'lei tsedek. Sh'ei bir'kat b'nei Aaron. Birshut ḥaveiray, n'vareikh Eloheinu shehasim'ḥah bim'ono v'she-akha'lenu mishelo.

Banish sickness and anger, so that even the unlearned will sing out with joy! Direct us onto the right paths. Accept the blessing of the sons of Aaron. With your permission Friends, let us shout with joy, blessing God in this celebration for the bounty we have shared.

(Those around the table respond and then the Leader repeats)

בָּרוּךְ אֱלֹהֵינוּ שֶׁהַשִּׂמְחָה בִּמְעוֹנוֹ וְשֶׁאָכַלְנוּ מִשֶּׁלּוֹ וּבְטוּבוֹ חָיִינוּ.

Barukh (Eloheinu) shehasim'ḥah bim'ono v'she-akha'lenu mishelo uv'tuvo ḥayinu.

Blessed is our God in whose presence we celebrate, for the bounty we have shared, and whose goodness is upon our life.

(Together)

Barukh hu uvarukh sh'mo בָּרוּךְ הוּא וּבָרוּךְ שְׁמוֹ.

Blessed is He and blessed is His Name!

(Turn to page 31 to continue Birkat. Return to page 49 for the Sheva B'rakhot)

Sheva B'rakhot for Wedding Meal

(Immediately after reciting Birkat HaMazon at a wedding meal, the first six blessings below are recited over a cup of wine by friends and relatives, the cup being passed to those reciting the blessing)

1 בָּרוּךְ אַתָּה יְיָ אֱלֹהֵינוּ מֶלֶךְ הָעוֹלָם, שֶׁהַכֹּל בָּרָא לִכְבוֹדוֹ.

Barukh atah Adonai Eloheinu Melekh Ha'Olam, she'hakol bara likh'vodo.

Blessed are you, Lord our God, King of the Universe, who created everything for His glory.

2 בָּרוּךְ אַתָּה יְיָ אֱלֹהֵינוּ מֶלֶךְ הָעוֹלָם, יוֹצֵר הָאָדָם.

Barukh atah Adonai Eloheinu Melekh Ha'Olam, yotseir ha'adam.

Blessed are you, Lord our God, King of the Universe, who created humanity.

3 בָּרוּךְ אַתָּה יְיָ אֱלֹהֵינוּ מֶלֶךְ הָעוֹלָם, אֲשֶׁר יָצַר
אֶת־הָאָדָם בְּצַלְמוֹ, בְּצֶלֶם דְּמוּת תַּבְנִיתוֹ וְהִתְקִין לוֹ מִמֶּנּוּ
בִּנְיַן עֲדֵי עַד. בָּרוּךְ אַתָּה יְיָ, יוֹצֵר הָאָדָם.

Barukh atah Adonai Eloheinu Melekh Ha'Olam, asher yatsar et ha'adam b'tsalmo b'tselem d'mut tavnito v'hitkin lo mimenu binyan adei ad. Barukh ata Adonai, yotseir ha'adam.

Blessed are you, Lord our God, King of the Universe, who created humanity in His image, in the image of the likeness of his form, and made for them an everlasting establishment. Blessed are you, Lord, who created humanity.

4 שׂוֹשׂ תָּשִׂישׂ וְתָגֵל הָעֲקָרָה בְּקִבּוּץ בָּנֶיהָ לְתוֹכָהּ בְּשִׂמְחָה.
בָּרוּךְ אַתָּה יְיָ, מְשַׂמֵּחַ צִיּוֹן בְּבָנֶיהָ.

Sos tasis v'tageil ha'akarah b'kibbuts bane'ha l'tokhah b'simḥah. Barukh ata Adonai, m'samei'aḥ Tsiyon b'vaneha.

May the barren one rejoice greatly and delight in the ingathering of her children within her in joy. Blessed are you Lord, who causes Tsiyon to rejoice with her children.

5 שַׂמֵּחַ תְּשַׂמַּח רֵעִים הָאֲהוּבִים כְּשַׂמֵּחֲךָ יְצִירְךָ בְּגַן עֵדֶן
מִקֶּדֶם. בָּרוּךְ אַתָּה יְיָ, מְשַׂמֵּחַ חָתָן וְכַלָּה.

Samei-aḥ t'samaḥ rei'im ha'ahuvim k'samei-ḥa-kha yetsir'kha b'gan eden mikedem. Barukh ata Adonai, m'samei-aḥ ḥatan v'khalah.

May the loving couple rejoice as You caused those You created to delight in the Garden of Eden of old. Blessed are You, Lord, who causes the groom and bride to rejoice.

6 בָּרוּךְ אַתָּה יְיָ אֱלֹהֵינוּ מֶלֶךְ הָעוֹלָם, אֲשֶׁר בָּרָא שָׂשׂוֹן
וְשִׂמְחָה, חָתָן וְכַלָּה, גִּילָה, רִנָּה, דִּיצָה וְחֶדְוָה, אַהֲבָה וְאַחֲוָה
וְשָׁלוֹם וְרֵעוּת. מְהֵרָה, יְיָ אֱלֹהֵינוּ, יִשָּׁמַע בְּעָרֵי יְהוּדָה
וּבְחֻצוֹת יְרוּשָׁלָיִם, קוֹל שָׂשׂוֹן וְקוֹל שִׂמְחָה, קוֹל חָתָן וְקוֹל
כַּלָּה, קוֹל מִצְהֲלוֹת חֲתָנִים מֵחֻפָּתָם וּנְעָרִים מִמִּשְׁתֵּה
נְגִינָתָם. בָּרוּךְ אַתָּה יְיָ, מְשַׂמֵּחַ חָתָן עִם הַכַּלָּה.

Barukh atah Adonai Eloheinu Melekh Ha'Olam, asher bara sason v'simḥa ḥatan v'khalah, gilah, rinah, ditsah v'ḥedvah, ahavah v'aḥavah v'shalom v'rei'ut. M'heirah, Adonai Eloheinu, yishama b'arei Yehudah u'veḥutsot Yerushalayim, kol sason v'kol simḥah, kol ḥatan v'kol kalah, kol mits-halot ḥa'tanim meiḥupatam u'ne'arim mimish'teih n'ginatam. Barukh ata Adonai m'sameiaḥ ḥatan im ha'kalah.

Blessed are You Lord our God, King of the Universe, who creates happiness and joy, groom and bride, exultation, delight, amusement, and pleasure, love and brotherhood, peace and friendship. Soon, Lord our God, may the sound of happiness and the sound of joy and the voice of the groom and the voice of the bride be heard in the cities of Judah and in the streets of Jerusalem, the rejoicing of the groom and the rejoicing of the bride from their huppahs and the young people at their banquets. Blessed are You Lord, who makes the groom rejoice with the bride.

7 בָּרוּךְ אַתָּה יְיָ אֱלֹהֵינוּ מֶלֶךְ הָעוֹלָם בּוֹרֵא פְּרִי הַגָּפֶן.

Barukh atah Adonai Eloheinu Melekh Ha'Olam, borei p'ri ha'gafen.

Blessed are You, Lord our God, King of the Universe, who creates the fruit of the vine.

(Wine from both of the two cups of wine are poured into the empty cup, and then some of the wine in the third cup is poured back into the two other cups. The bride drinks one cup, the group drinks another cup, and the Leader of Birkat HaMazon drinks the remaining cup)

Havdalah

(At the conclusion of Shabbat, a Havdalah candle is lit and the following is recited. At the conclusion of a Festival, recite only the blessing over wine and the final blessing; omit the items and blessings for spices and candle)

הִנֵּה אֵל יְשׁוּעָתִי, אֶבְטַח וְלֹא אֶפְחָד, כִּי עָזִּי וְזִמְרָת יָהּ יְיָ, וַיְהִי לִי לִישׁוּעָה. וּשְׁאַבְתֶּם מַיִם בְּשָׂשׂוֹן מִמַּעַיְנֵי הַיְשׁוּעָה. לַיְיָ הַיְשׁוּעָה עַל עַמְּךָ בִרְכָתֶךָ. יְיָ צְבָאוֹת עִמָּנוּ מִשְׂגָּב לָנוּ אֱלֹהֵי יַעֲקֹב. יְיָ צְבָאוֹת אַשְׁרֵי אָדָם בֹּטֵחַ בָּךְ. יְיָ הוֹשִׁיעָה הַמֶּלֶךְ יַעֲנֵנוּ בְיוֹם קָרְאֵנוּ. לַיְּהוּדִים הָיְתָה אוֹרָה וְשִׂמְחָה וְשָׂשׂוֹן וִיקָר. כֵּן תִּהְיֶה לָּנוּ, כּוֹס יְשׁוּעוֹת אֶשָּׂא. וּבְשֵׁם יְיָ אֶקְרָא.

Hinei El y'shuati, evtaḥ v'lo efḥad, ki ozi v'zimrat Yah Adonai, vay'hi li lishuah. Ush'avtem mayim b'sason mi-ma-ay'neiy ha'yeshuah. L'Adonai ha'yeshuah al am'kha vir'khatekha. Adonai Ts'vaot imanu misgav lanu, Elohei Yaakov. Adonai Ts'vaot, ashrei adam botei-aḥ bakh. Adonai hoshiah haMelekh ya'aneinu v'yom kar'einu. LaY'hudim hay'tah orah v'simḥah v'sason vikar. Kein tih'yeh lanu, kos yeshuot esa. Uv'sheim Adonai ekra.

Behold, God is my salvation; I will trust and will not be afraid, for God is my strength and my song; indeed, He has saved me. You will drink with joy from the waters of salvation; the salvation of the Lord. Your blessing be upon Your people. The Lord of Hosts is with us; the God of Jacob is our stronghold. Lord of Hosts, happy is the one who trusts in You. Lord, save us! May the King answer us when we call. To the Jews were given light and joy, gladness and honor; so may it be for us. I will raise up the cup of salvation, and call on the Name of the Lord.

(Recite the following over an overflowing cup of wine or grape juice and an already lit havdalah candle. The candle will be put out in the overflow)

בָּרוּךְ אַתָּה יְיָ, אֱלֹהֵינוּ מֶלֶךְ הָעוֹלָם, בּוֹרֵא פְּרִי הַגָּפֶן.

Barukh atah Adonai Eloheinu Melekh Ha'Olam, borei p'ri ha'gafen.

Blessed are You, Lord our God, King of the Universe, who creates the fruit of the vine.

(Recite the following over spices, which are then passed for each person to smell)

בָּרוּךְ אַתָּה יְיָ, אֱלֹהֵינוּ מֶלֶךְ הָעוֹלָם, בּוֹרֵא מִינֵי בְשָׂמִים.

Barukh atah Adonai Eloheinu Melekh Ha'Olam, borei minei v'samim.

Blessed are You, Lord our God, King of the Universe, who creates fragrant spices.

(Recite the following over the havdalah candle as people hold their hands out to see the lights reflection on their fingernails)

בָּרוּךְ אַתָּה יְיָ, אֱלֹהֵינוּ מֶלֶךְ הָעוֹלָם, בּוֹרֵא מְאוֹרֵי הָאֵשׁ.

Barukh atah Adonai Eloheinu Melekh Ha'Olam, borei me'orei ha'eish.

Blessed are You, Lord our God, King of the Universe, who creates the light of the fire.

(Continue)

בָּרוּךְ אַתָּה יְיָ, אֱלֹהֵינוּ מֶלֶךְ הָעוֹלָם, הַמַּבְדִיל בֵּין קֹדֶשׁ לְחוֹל, בֵּין אוֹר לְחֹשֶׁךְ, בֵּין יִשְׂרָאֵל לָעַמִּים, בֵּין יוֹם הַשְּׁבִיעִי, לְשֵׁשֶׁת יְמֵי הַמַּעֲשֶׂה.

Barukh atah Adonai Eloheinu Melekh Ha'Olam, hamav'dil bein kodesh l'ḥol, bein ohr l'ḥoshekh, bein Yisraeil la'amim, bein yom hashvi'i, l'sheishet y'mei hama'aseh.

Blessed are You, Lord our God, King of the Universe, You have made a distinction between that which is holy and that which is common; between light and darkness; between Israel and the other nations; between the seventh day and the six days of work.

בָּרוּךְ אַתָּה יְיָ, הַמַּבְדִּיל בֵּין קֹדֶשׁ לְחוֹל.

Barukh atah Adonai, ha'mavdil bein kodesh l'ḥol.

Blessed are You, Lord, who has made a distinction between the holy and the profane.

(The cup is drunk and the Havdalah candle is extinguished in the spilled wine or grape juice from the cup)

Eliyahu

אֵלִיָּהוּ הַנָּבִיא, אֵלִיָּהוּ הַתִּשְׁבִּי, אֵלִיָּהוּ הַגִּלְעָדִי.
בִּמְהֵרָה בְיָמֵינוּ, יָבֹא אֵלֵינוּ, עִם מָשִׁיחַ יֵשׁוּעַ בֶּן דָּוִד.

Eiliyahu haNavi, Eiliyahu haTishbi, Eiliyahu haGiladi. Bim'heirah ve'yameinu yavo eileinu, im Mashiaḥ Yeishua ben David.

May Elijah the Prophet, Elijah of the Tishbi, Elijah of the Giladi: Come to us in our days proclaiming redemption, and with him Messiah Yeshua son of David.

Ha'Mavdil bein Kodesh

הַמַּבְדִּיל בֵּין קֹדֶשׁ לְחֹל חַטֹּאתֵינוּ הוּא יִמְחֹל;
זַרְעֵנוּ וְכַסְפֵּנוּ יַרְבֶּה כַּחוֹל וְכַכּוֹכָבִים בַּלָּיְלָה.
שָׁבֻעַ טוֹב...

May He who distinguishes between the holy and the profane forgive our sin; may our offspring and our means be as the sand and as the stars in the night. May it be a good week!

יוֹם פָּנָה כְּצֵל תֹּמֶר אֶקְרָא לָאֵל עָלַי גֹּמֵר;
אָמַר שׁוֹמֵר אָתָא בֹקֶר וְגַם לָיְלָה.
שָׁבֻעַ טוֹב...

The day has turned as the shadow of the date palm, I shall call upon God to fulfill His promise to me; the Watchman has said, "Morning has come with the night." May it be a good week!

קְרָאתִיךָ יָהּ הוֹשִׁיעֵנִי אֹרַח חַיִּים תּוֹדִיעֵנִי;
מִדַּלָּה תְבַצְּעֵנִי מִיּוֹם עַד לָיְלָה.
שָׁבֻעַ טוֹב...

God, I called upon You and You rescued me. Declare to me the
way of life. Quickly bring to an end my poverty,
as from the day to the night. May it be a good week!

נַחְנוּ בְיָדְךָ כַּחֹמֶר סְלַח נָא עַל קַל וָחֹמֶר;
יוֹם לְיוֹם יַבִּיעַ אֹמֶר וְלַיְלָה לְלָיְלָה.
שָׁבֻעַ טוֹב...

We are like clay in Your hand. Please forgive us, we are but clay,
both great and small. Day after day and night after night
this word shall be poured forth. May it be a good week!

הַמַּבְדִּיל בֵּין קֹדֶשׁ לְחֹל חַטֹּאתֵינוּ הוּא יִמְחֹל;
זַרְעֵנוּ וְכַסְפֵּנוּ יַרְבֶּה כַּחוֹל וְכַכּוֹכָבִים בַּלָּיְלָה.
שָׁבֻעַ טוֹב...

May He who distinguishes between the holy and the profane
forgive our sin; may our offspring and our means be as
the sand and as the stars in the night. May it be a good week!

Holiday Blessings & Readings

Blessings for Taking Up the Lulav on Sukkot

יְהִי רָצוֹן מִלְּפָנֶיךָ, יְיָ אֱלֹהַי וֵאלֹהֵי אֲבוֹתַי, בִּפְרִי עֵץ הָדָר, וְכַפּוֹת תְּמָרִים, וַעֲנַף עֵץ עָבוֹת, וְעַרְבֵי נָחַל, אוֹתִיּוֹת שִׁמְךָ. בְּרִיךְ הוּא וּשְׁכִינְתֵּהּ, בִּדְחִילוּ וּרְחִימוּ, לְיַחֵד שֵׁם, בְּשֵׁם כָּל יִשְׂרָאֵל. אָמֵן. בָּרוּךְ יְיָ לְעוֹלָם, אָמֵן וְאָמֵן.

May it be Your will, Lord my God and God of my Fathers, that through my taking up the fruit of the etrog tree, the date palm branches, the branches of the myrtle and willow, that I seek Your name. Blessed are You and Your presence in this world. In awe and in love do we seek to make holy Your name as Your people Israel. Blessed is the Lord forever and ever. Amen and amen.

Proper procedure for taking up the Lulav and Etrog

It is a mitsvah to wave the lulav on each of the first seven days of Sukkot, although not on Shabbat according to Jewish tradition due to a general Rabbinic prohibition against carrying on Shabbat. Some communities do wave lulav on Shabbat so consult your Rabbi for your community's custom.

The lulav is assembled as follows: hold the lulav with the spine side (smooth side) facing toward you, then place the two branches of aravah (willow) in the left side holder of the lulav and the three branches of hadas (myrtle) in the right holder. The hadas should sit slightly higher on the lulav than the aravah.

The proper time to take up the lulav is in the morning, both in one's own sukkah and during the special Sukkot liturgy in the morning service. While reciting the blessing below, the etrog is held with the pittam (stem) pointed down in the left hand. The lulav is held in the right hand. After reciting the blessing, the etrog is turned around so that it is held with the pittam facing up

בָּרוּךְ אַתָּה יְיָ אֱלֹהֵינוּ מֶלֶךְ הָעוֹלָם, אֲשֶׁר קִדְּשָׁנוּ בְּמִצְוֹתָיו, וְצִוָּנוּ עַל נְטִילַת לוּלָב.

Barukh atah Adonai Eloheinu Melekh Ha'Olam,
asher kid'shanu b'mitsvotayv v'tsivanu al netilat lulav.

Blessed are You, Lord our God, King of the Universe, who has sanctified us with His commandments and has commanded us to take up the lulav.

(On the first use of the lulav for the year recite the Sheheheyanu blessing)

בָּרוּךְ אַתָּה יְיָ אֱלֹהֵינוּ מֶלֶךְ הָעוֹלָם, שֶׁהֶחֱיָנוּ, וְקִיְּמָנוּ,
וְהִגִּיעָנוּ, לַזְּמַן הַזֶּה.

Barukh atah Adonai Eloheinu Melekh Ha'Olam, sheheḥeyanu, vekiyemanu, vehigiyanu, lazman hazeh!

Blessed are You, Lord our God, King of the Universe, who has kept us, and sustained us, and enabled us to reach this season!

(After the blessing you wave/shake the lulav in the following manner)

- Stand facing east.

- Hold the lulav out to the east (in front of you) and shake it three times. Each time the motion of shaking should be a drawing in to you: *reach out and draw in, reach out and draw in, reach out and draw in.*

- Repeat the same motion three times to your right (south), behind and over your shoulder (west), to your left (north), raising it up above you (the heavens), and lowering it down toward your feet (the earth).

- All of these should be done slowly and deliberately concentrating on the symbolism and intention of the act.

The lulav is also waved during the Hallel liturgy while saying the verse:

הוֹדוּ לַייָ כִּי טוֹב, כִּי לְעוֹלָם חַסְדּוֹ.

Hodu l'Adonai ki tov, ki l'olam ḥasdo.

Give thanks to God, for God is good, for God's lovingkindness endures forever.

Hodu – shake front [East] – הוֹדוּ

L'Adonai – Pause, Don't shake when saying God's name! – לַיְיָ

Ki – shake right [South] – כִּי

Tov – shake back [West] – טוֹב

Ki – shake left [North] – כִּי

L'olam - shake up – לְעוֹלָם

ḥasdo - shake down – חַסְדּוֹ

The lulav is again waved similiarly while saying:

יֹאמַר נָא יִשְׂרָאֵל, כִּי לְעוֹלָם חַסְדּוֹ.

Yomar Na Yisraeil, ki l'olam ḥasdo

Let Israel say that God's lovingkindness endures forever.

The lulav is again waved similiarly while saying:

אָנָּא יְיָ הוֹשִׁיעָה נָּא.

Ana Adonai hoshiah na
We beg Lord, please save us now!

אָנָּא יְיָ הַצְלִיחָה נָא.

Ana Adonai hats'liḥa na
We beg Lord, please prosper us now!

Purim

(Recite the following blessings before reading Megillat Esther)

בָּרוּךְ אַתָּה יְיָ אֱלֹהֵינוּ מֶלֶךְ הָעוֹלָם, אֲשֶׁר קִדְּשָׁנוּ בְּמִצְוֹתָיו וְצִוָּנוּ עַל מִקְרָא מְגִלָּה.

Barukh atah Adonai, Eloheinu Melekh Ha'Olam, asher kid'shanu b'mitsvotayv, v'tsivanu al mikrah megillah.

Blessed are You, Lord our God, King of the Universe, who sanctifies us by His commandments and who has commanded us to read the Megillah.

בָּרוּךְ אַתָּה יְיָ אֱלֹהֵינוּ מֶלֶךְ הָעוֹלָם, שֶׁעָשָׂה נִסִּים לַאֲבוֹתֵינוּ בַּיָּמִים הָהֵם, בַּזְּמַן הַזֶּה.

Barukh atah Adonai Eloheinu Melekh Ha'Olam, she-asa nisim la-voteinu, ba-yamim ha-hem, bazman ha-zeh.

Blessed are You, Lord our God, King of the Universe, who has done miraculous deeds for our forefathers, in those days at this season.

בָּרוּךְ אַתָּה יְיָ אֱלֹהֵינוּ מֶלֶךְ הָעוֹלָם, שֶׁהֶחֱיָנוּ, וְקִיְּמָנוּ, וְהִגִּיעָנוּ, לַזְּמַן הַזֶּה.

Barukh atah Adonai Eloheinu Melekh Ha'Olam, sheheḥeyanu, vekiyemanu, vehigiyanu, lazman hazeh!

Blessed are You, Lord our God, King of the Universe, who has kept us, and sustained us, and enabled us to reach this season!

(Recite the following after reading Megillat Esther; Hebrew on pages 32 & 34)

We thank you for the miracles, for the redemption, for the mighty deeds, for the saving acts, and for the battles which You have done for our ancestors in those days, at this time.

In the days of Mordecai and Esther, in the capital city of Shushan, when the wicked Haman stood against them, asking that all the Jews be annihilated, murdered, and destroyed, both young and old, infants and women, and to take their plunder, in one day, on the thirteenth day of the twelfth month, which is Adar. You, in Your great compassion, annulled this decree, spoiling his purposes, and returning to him judgement upon his own head, that both he and his sons would hang upon the tree.

Blessing for the Counting of the Omer

בָּרוּךְ אַתָּה יְיָ אֱלֹהֵינוּ מֶלֶךְ הָעוֹלָם, אֲשֶׁר קִדְּשָׁנוּ בְּמִצְוֹתָיו,
וְצִוָּנוּ עַל סְפִירַת הָעוֹמֶר.

Barukh atah Adonai Eloheinu Melekh Ha'Olam, asher kid'shanu b'mitsvotayv v'tsivanu al sefirat haOmer.

Blessed are You, Lord our God, King of the Universe, who sanctifies us by His commandments and who has commanded us to count the Omer.

(For the first week you count just the days. After a complete week, you count both the number of days and the number of weeks)

Today is __________ (total) day(s), which are _______ week(s) and ________ day(s), of the Omer.

Shavuot: When to start counting?

Shavuot is an important holiday for Jews. Jewish tradition holds that God gave us the Torah on Shavuot. Shavuot is the climax that Passover builds up to. Because of this, it is important that we get the timing right. Leviticus 23:15 tells us to start counting "From the day after the Shabbat," but which Shabbat?

Jewish traditions differ in their interpretations of "the Shabbat." In the Second Temple Period, the Sadducees, Essenes, and Samaritans began counting toward Shavuot on the Sunday either during Passover or after the end of Passover. This is because they read "the Shabbat" to be literally the Seventh Day Shabbat and not the Passover days as Shabbatot. The Essenes used a solar calendar, adding further variation to the calculation of dates; other Jewish religious groups used a lunar calendar. To this day, the small community of Samaritans in Israel make a pilgrimage to Mount Gerizim, counting Shavuot by their ancient method.

Karaite Judaism, a sect of Judaism that grew in the middle ages, sought to make biblical interpretations that focused on the text rather than Rabbinic tradition. Karaite Jews read "the Shabbat" to mean the Shabbat that is observed during the Passover week.

Beta Israel, the community of Ethiopian Jews, understands "the Shabbat" as being the seventh day of Passover, which is Biblically a special Yom Tov and is treated like a Shabbat day. This tradition likely goes back to pre-Rabbinic times, as Beta Israel is a Jewish community with ancient roots.

The Rabbinic tradition, with which most Jews are familiar, reads "the Shabbat" as the first day of Passover, which is also a Yom Tov. Thus, Rabbinic tradition begins counting toward Shavuot during Passover. The Rabbinic tradition is not by any means the most intuitive interpretation of the Biblical commandment, but it nevertheless defers to the text as well.

The Second Temple period saw much Jewish sectarianism. Some persists today, but the overwhelming majority of the Jewish community follows the Rabbinic tradition. The Rabbinic tradition stretches back to the Pharisees and is attested by the first-century Jewish historians Philo and Josephus. In all likelihood, Messiah Yeshua and Paul followed this tradition, as they worked within the Pharisaic milieu. At Devar Emet Messianic Publications, we do not assume to know which tradition is right. (Because every harvest season is different, the Biblical commandment most likely came with some leeway as to the exact date on which to begin counting – see Deuteronomy 16:9–12.)

In alignment with our value at Devar Emet of respecting Jewish tradition, for the sake of holiday unity with the overwhelming majority of the Jewish community and because Messiah Yeshua seemed to generally associate himself with the Pharisaic tradition, Devar Emet follows the Pharisaic-Rabbinic tradition of counting toward Shavuot starting with Passover and encourages you to do likewise.

Ḥanukah

(Using the lit shammash candle, light each new candle first, starting on the extreme right of the Ḥanukah Menorah, as you are facing it, on the first night, then adding the daily candle to the left of the previous night's candle, thus lighting the candles from left to right, while reciting the following blessings. On Erev Shabbat light the Ḥanukah Menorah before the Shabbat candles. On Saturday night traditions vary whether to light the Havdalah candle before the Ḥanukah Menorah or afterward. Maoz Tsur is traditionally sung each night of Ḥanukah)

בָּרוּךְ אַתָּה יְיָ אֱלֹהֵינוּ מֶלֶךְ הָעוֹלָם, אֲשֶׁר קִדְּשָׁנוּ בְּמִצְוֹתָיו, וְצִוָּנוּ לְהַדְלִיק נֵר שֶׁל חֲנֻכָּה.

Barukh atah Adonai Eloheinu Melekh Ha'Olam, asher kid'shanu be-mitsvotayv, v'tsivanu l'hadlik neir shel Ḥanukah.

Blessed are You, Lord our God, King of the Universe, who has sanctified us with His commandments, and commanded us to light the Ḥanukah lights.

בָּרוּךְ אַתָּה יְיָ אֱלֹהֵינוּ מֶלֶךְ הָעוֹלָם, שֶׁעָשָׂה נִסִּים לַאֲבוֹתֵינוּ בַּיָּמִים הָהֵם בַּזְּמַן הַזֶּה.

Barukh atah Adonai, Eloheinu Melekh Ha'Olam, she'asah nisim la'avoteinu ba'yamim ha-heim baz'man hazeh.

Blessed are You, Lord our God, King of the Universe who has done miraculous deeds for our forefathers, in those days at this season.

(Only Recite on the First Night of Ḥanukah)

בָּרוּךְ אַתָּה יְיָ אֱלֹהֵינוּ מֶלֶךְ הָעוֹלָם, שֶׁהֶחֱיָנוּ, וְקִיְּמָנוּ, וְהִגִּיעָנוּ, לַזְּמַן הַזֶּה.

Barukh atah Adonai Eloheinu Melekh Ha'Olam, sheheḥeyanu, vekiyemanu, vehigiyanu, lazman hazeh!

Blessed are You, Lord our God, King of the Universe, who has kept us, and sustained us, and enabled us to reach this season!

John 8:12

הַמָּשִׁיחַ יֵשׁוּעַ הוֹסִיף לְדַבֵּר אֲלֵיהֶם וְאָמַר: "אֲנִי אוֹר הָעוֹלָם. אִישׁ הַהוֹלֵךְ אַחֲרַי לֹא יִתְהַלֵּךְ בַּחֹשֶׁךְ, אֶלָּא אוֹר הַחַיִּים יִהְיֶה לוֹ."

Messiah Yeshua spoke unto them, saying: "I am the light of the world. A person that follows after me shall not walk in the darkness, but shall have the light of life."

Blessing of the Light of Messiah Yeshua

בָּרוּךְ אַתָּה יְיָ אֱלֹהֵינוּ מֶלֶךְ הָעוֹלָם, אֲשֶׁר קִדְּשָׁנוּ בִּדְבָרוֹ, וְנָתַן לָנוּ אֶת יֵשׁוּעַ מְשִׁיחֵנוּ, אוֹר הָעוֹלָם.

Barukh atah Adonai Eloheinu Melekh Ha'Olam, asher kid'shanu bidvaro, v'natan lanu et Yeishua Meshiḥeinu, Or ha'Olam.

Blessed are You, Lord our God, King of the Universe, who has sanctified us with his word, and has given us Yeshua our Messiah, the Light of the World.

עַל הַנִּסִּים וְעַל הַפֻּרְקָן, וְעַל הַגְּבוּרוֹת, וְעַל הַתְּשׁוּעוֹת וְעַל הַמִּלְחָמוֹת שֶׁעָשִׂיתָ לַאֲבוֹתֵינוּ בַּיָּמִים הָהֵם בַּזְּמַן הַזֶּה.

Al hanisim v'al hapurkan, v'al hag'vurot, v'al hat'shu-ot, v'al hamil'ḥamot sheh-asitah la'avoteinu bayameem haheim baz'man hazeh.

We thank you for the miracles, for the redemption, for the mighty deeds, for the saving acts, and for the battles which You have done for our ancestors in those days, at this time.

בִּימֵי מַתִּתְיָהוּ בֶּן יוֹחָנָן כֹּהֵן גָּדוֹל, חַשְׁמוֹנַי וּבָנָיו, כְּשֶׁעָמְדָה מַלְכוּת יָוָן הָרְשָׁעָה עַל עַמְּךָ יִשְׂרָאֵל לְהַשְׁכִּיחָם תּוֹרָתֶךָ, וּלְהַעֲבִירָם מֵחֻקֵּי רְצוֹנֶךָ. וְאַתָּה בְּרַחֲמֶיךָ הָרַבִּים עָמַדְתָּ לָהֶם בְּעֵת צָרָתָם, רַבְתָּ אֶת רִיבָם, דַּנְתָּ אֶת דִּינָם, נָקַמְתָּ אֶת נִקְמָתָם, מָסַרְתָּ גִבּוֹרִים בְּיַד חַלָּשִׁים, וְרַבִּים בְּיַד

מְעַטִּים, וּטְמֵאִים בְּיַד טְהוֹרִים, וּרְשָׁעִים בְּיַד צַדִּיקִים, וְזֵדִים
בְּיַד עוֹסְקֵי תוֹרָתֶךָ. וּלְךָ עָשִׂיתָ שֵׁם גָּדוֹל וְקָדוֹשׁ בְּעוֹלָמֶךָ,
וּלְעַמְּךָ יִשְׂרָאֵל עָשִׂיתָ תְּשׁוּעָה גְדוֹלָה וּפֻרְקָן כְּהַיּוֹם הַזֶּה.
וְאַחַר כֵּן בָּאוּ בָנֶיךָ לִדְבִיר בֵּיתֶךָ, וּפִנּוּ אֶת הֵיכָלֶךָ, וְטִהֲרוּ
אֶת מִקְדָּשֶׁךָ, וְהִדְלִיקוּ נֵרוֹת בְּחַצְרוֹת קָדְשֶׁךָ, וְקָבְעוּ
שְׁמוֹנַת יְמֵי חֲנֻכָּה אֵלּוּ, לְהוֹדוֹת וּלְהַלֵּל לְשִׁמְךָ הַגָּדוֹל,
וּבְעֵת רְצוֹנְךָ שָׁלַחְתָּ לָנוּ אֶת־יֵשׁוּעַ מְשִׁיחֵנוּ, אוֹר הָעוֹלָם.

In the days of the Hasmonean Matityahu son of Yoḥanan the High Priest, and his sons, when stood the wicked kingdom of the Hellenists against Your people Israel to cause them to abandon Your Torah and to turn from the statutes of your will, You in Your great compassion stood for them in their time of tribulation. You contended for them in their fight, judged for them in their judgment, avenged them in their vengeance, and delivered them by means of heroes when they were weak; the many into the hands of the few, the unclean into the hands of the clean, the wicked into the hands of the righteous, and the deceiver into the hands of those who practiced Your Torah. Your great and holy Name is established in Your world, and You have established a great salvation for Your people Israel, and have redeemed them from that day to this. Indeed, after this Your children came into the holy place of Your house, we cleared Your Temple of defilement, and purified Your holy sanctuary, and lit the lights in Your holy court, and established the lighting of the lights in the eight days of Ḥanukah, to thank and to praise the greatness of Your Name, and at the time pleasing to You, sent Yeshua, our Messiah, the Light of the World.

Ma'oz Tsur

מָעוֹז צוּר יְשׁוּעָתִי לְךָ נָאֶה לְשַׁבֵּחַ,
תִּכּוֹן בֵּית תְּפִלָּתִי וְשָׁם תּוֹדָה נְזַבֵּחַ,
לְעֵת תָּכִין מַטְבֵּחַ מִצָּר הַמְנַבֵּחַ,
אָז אֶגְמֹר בְּשִׁיר מִזְמוֹר חֲנֻכַּת הַמִּזְבֵּחַ.

Ma'oz tsur Yeshuati, lekha na'eh le-shabei'aḥ,
Tikon beit tefilati, vesham todah nezabei'aḥ,
Le'eit takhin matbei'aḥ, mitsar hamna-bei'aḥ
Az egmor beshir mizmor, ḥanukat hamiz-bei'aḥ

Rock of Ages let our song praise your saving power
You amidst the raging foes, was our sheltering tower
Furious they assailed us, but Your arm availed us
And Your word broke their sword
when our own strength failed us

Rock of Ages, stumbling stone, whom the builders rejected
You've become the cornerstone, whom the Lord selected
Lift Yeshua up and praise Him, worship God who raised Him
Shine His light through the night, til the day we gaze on Him

(**Strict Translation of the first verse**: *A Refuge, my Rock of Salvation, it is pleasant to sing Your praises. Let our house of prayer be restored, and there we will offer You thanks. When You have slaughtered the cursing foe, then we will celebrate with song and psalm the altar's dedication.)*

Songs for Shabbat & Other Occasions

Al Hanisim

עַל הַנִּסִּים וְעַל הַפֻּרְקָן, וְעַל הַגְּבוּרוֹת, וְעַל הַתְּשׁוּעוֹת וְעַל
הַמִּלְחָמוֹת שֶׁעָשִׂיתָ לַאֲבוֹתֵינוּ בַּיָּמִים הָהֵם בַּזְּמַן הַזֶּה.

Al hanisim v'al hapurkan, v'al hag'vurot, v'al hat'shu-ot,
v'al hamil'ḥamot sheh-asitah la'avoteinu
bayameem haheim baz'man hazeh.

We thank you for the miracles, for the redemption, for the mighty deeds, for the saving acts, and for the battles which You have done for our ancestors in those days, at this time.

Am Yisrael Chai

עַם יִשְׂרָאֵל חַי! עוֹד אָבִינוּ חַי!

Am Yisraeil ḥai! Od Avinu ḥai!

The People of Israel live! Our Father lives!

David Melekh Yisrael

דָּוִד מֶלֶךְ יִשְׂרָאֵל חַי חַי וְקַיָּם

Da'vid Melekh Yisraeil ḥai ḥai v'kayam.

David, the King of Israel, lives on in the hearts of our people.

Esa Einai

אֶשָּׂא עֵינַי, אֶל הֶהָרִים, מֵאַיִן יָבֹא עֶזְרִי.
עֶזְרִי מֵעִם יְיָ עֹשֵׂה שָׁמַיִם וָאָרֶץ.
הִנֵּה לֹא יָנוּם, וְלֹא יִישָׁן שׁוֹמֵר יִשְׂרָאֵל.

Esah einai el heharim, mei'ayin yavo ezri.
Ezri me'im Adonai oseih shamayim va'aretz.
Hineih lo yanum, v'lo yishan Shomeir Yisraeil.

I lift my eyes up to the mountains, from where my help comes.
My help comes from the Lord who made the heavens and the earth.
Behold, The Guardian of Israel neither slumbers nor sleeps.

HaMalakh HaGoel

הַמַּלְאָךְ הַגֹּאֵל אֹתִי מִכָּל-רָע, יְבָרֵךְ אֶת-הַנְּעָרִים,
וְיִקָּרֵא בָהֶם שְׁמִי,
וְשֵׁם אֲבֹתַי אַבְרָהָם וְיִצְחָק, וְיִדְגּוּ לָרֹב בְּקֶרֶב הָאָרֶץ.

Hamalakh hagoeil oti mikhal ra, yevareikh et ha-ne'arim,
v'yikareih bahem sh'mi, v'sheim avotai Avraham v'Yitsḥak,
v'yidgu larov b'kerev ha'arets.

May the angel who has redeemed me from all evil, bless the youth; and let my name be named in them, and the name of my fathers Abraham and Isaac; and let them grow into a multitude in the midst of the earth.

HaTikvah

כָּל עוֹד בַּלֵּבָב פְּנִימָה, נֶפֶשׁ יְהוּדִי הוֹמִיָּה,
וּלְפַאֲתֵי מִזְרָח קָדִימָה, עַיִן לְצִיּוֹן צוֹפִיָּה.
עוֹד לֹא אָבְדָה תִּקְוָתֵנוּ, הַתִּקְוָה בַּת שְׁנוֹת אַלְפַּיִם,
לִהְיוֹת עַם חָפְשִׁי בְּאַרְצֵנוּ אֶרֶץ צִיּוֹן וִירוּשָׁלַיִם.

Kol od beleivav penimah, nefesh Yehudi homi'yah,
Ul'fatei miz'raḥ kadimah, ayin l'Tsiyon tsofi'yah,
Od lo avdah tik'vateinu, ha'tikvah bat shnot al'payim,
Lih'yot am ḥafshi b'artseinu erets Tsiyon vi'rushalayim.

As long as in the inner heart, a Jewish soul still yearns,
And to the edges of the east, forward, an eye towards Tsiyon still looks,
Our hope has still not been lost, the hope of two thousand years,
To be a free nation in our land, the land of Tsiyon and Jerusalem.

Hava Nagila

הָבָה נָגִילָה, הָבָה נָגִילָה, הָבָה נָגִילָה וְנִשְׂמְחָה!
הָבָה נְרַנְּנָה, הָבָה נְרַנְּנָה, הָבָה נְרַנְּנָה וְנִשְׂמְחָה!
עוּרוּ, עוּרוּ אַחִים,
עוּרוּ אַחִים בְּלֵב שָׂמֵחַ!

Hava nagila, hava nagila, Hava nagila ve-nismeḥah!
Hava neranena, hava neranena, Hava neranena, ve-nismeḥah!
'Uru, 'uru 'aḥim, 'Uru 'aḥim be-leiv samei'aḥ!

Come on, let's rejoice, come on, let's rejoice,
Come on, let's rejoice and be happy!
Come on, let's exult, come on, let's exult, Come on, let's exult and be happy!
Wake up, wake up, brothers! Wake up, brothers, with a happy heart!

HaYom Yom Shishi

הַיּוֹם יוֹם שִׁשִּׁי, הַיּוֹם יוֹם שִׁשִּׁי.
מָחָר שַׁבָּת, מָחָר שַׁבָּת. שַׁבָּת מְנוּחָה.

הַיּוֹם כּוּלָּם עוֹבְדִים, הַיּוֹם כּוּלָּם עוֹבְדִים.
מָחָר שַׁבָּת, מָחָר שַׁבָּת. שַׁבָּת מְנוּחָה.

HaYom Yom Shishi, HaYom Shishi
Maḥar Shabbat, Maḥar Shabbat, Shabbat m'nuḥah

Hayom kulam ov'dim, Hayom kulam ov'dim
Maḥar Shabbat, Maḥar Shabbat, Shabbat m'nuḥah

Today is Friday. Today is Friday.
Tomorrow is Shabbat, tomorrow is Shabbat, restful Shabbat.
Today everyone works. Today everyone works.
Tomorrow is Shabbat, tomorrow is Shabbat, restful Shabbat.

Heiveinu Shalom Aleikhem

Heiveinu Shalom Aleikhem — הֵבֵאנוּ שָׁלוֹם עֲלֵיכֶם

Heiveinu Shalom Aleikhem — הֵבֵאנוּ שָׁלוֹם עֲלֵיכֶם

Heiveinu Shalom Aleikhem — הֵבֵאנוּ שָׁלוֹם עֲלֵיכֶם

הֵבֵאנוּ שָׁלוֹם שָׁלוֹם שָׁלוֹם עֲלֵיכֶם

Heiveinu Shalom, Shalom, Shalom Aleikhem

This is my hope & my prayer, that there be peace everywhere,
that there be joy for all to share,
So let us praise our God and live a happy life.

Hineih MaTov

הִנֵּה מַה טּוֹב וּמַה נָּעִים שֶׁבֶת אַחִים גַּם יָחַד.

Hineih mah tov umah na'im shevet aḥim gam yaḥad.

Behold, how good and how pleasant it is for people to dwell together in unity!

Ivdu

עִבְדוּ אֶת יְיָ בְּשִׂמְחָה. בֹּאוּ לְפָנָיו בִּרְנָנָה.
כִּי טוֹב יְיָ לְעוֹלָם חַסְדּוֹ וְעַד דֹּר וָדֹר אֱמוּנָתוֹ.

Ivdu et Adonai besimḥa. Bo'u lefanav birnanah.
Ki tov Adonai l'olam ḥasdo v'ad dor vador emunato.

Serve the Lord with joyfulness! Come before Him with happiness.
For the Lord is good. His mercy endures forever
and His faithfulness unto all generations.

Ki Heim Ḥayeinu

כִּי הֵם חַיֵּינוּ וְאֹרֶךְ יָמֵינוּ, וּבָהֶם נֶהְגֶּה יוֹמָם וָלָיְלָה.
וְאַהֲבָתְךָ אַל תָּסִיר מִמֶּנּוּ לְעוֹלָמִים.

Ki heim ḥayeinu v'orekh yameinu u'va'hem neh'geh yomam va'laila. V'ahavt'kha al tasir mimenu le'olamin.

For they are our life and the length of our days, and we will meditate on them day and night. May you never take away your love from us.

Ko Amar

כֹּה אָמַר יְיָ, מָצָא חֵן בַּמִּדְבָּר עַם שְׂרִידֵי חָרֶב הָלוֹךְ לְהַרְגִּיעוֹ יִשְׂרָאֵל.

Kho amar Adonai, matsa ḥein bamidbar am shridei ḥarev halokh l'har-gi-o Yisraeil.

Thus says the Lord: the people that were left from the sword have found grace in the wilderness, even Israel, when I go to cause him to rest (Jeremiah 31:1)

L'khu N'ran'na

לְכוּ נְרַנְּנָה לַייָ נָרִיעָה, לְצוּר יִשְׁעֵנוּ.
נְקַדְּמָה פָנָיו בְּתוֹדָה בִּזְמִרוֹת נָרִיעַ לוֹ.

L'khu n'ranena l'Adonai nariah, l'tsur yisheinu.
N'kadmah fanayv b'todah biz'mirot naria lo.

O come, let us sing unto the Lord; let us shout for joy to the Rock of our salvation. Let us come before His presence with thanksgiving, let us shout for joy unto Him with songs.

Lo Ira

לֹא אִירָא מֵרִבְבוֹת עָם אֲשֶׁר סָבִיב סָבִיב שָׁתוּ עָלָי.
קוּמָה יְיָ. הוֹשִׁיעֵנִי.

Lo ira meriv'vot am asher saviv saviv shatu alai.
Kuma Adonai. Hoshi-eini.

I will not fear the multitudes that have set themselves against me.
Arise, O Lord! Save me!

Mayim

וּשְׁאַבְתֶּם מַיִם בְּשָׂשׂוֹן מִמַּעַיְנֵי הַיְשׁוּעָה.
מַיִם, מַיִם, מַיִם, מַיִם, הֵי מַיִם בְּשָׂשׂוֹן!
הֵי, הֵי, הֵי, הֵי,מַיִם, מַיִם,מַיִם, מַיִם ,מַיִם, מַיִם בְּשָׂשׂוֹן

U'sheav-tem mayim be'sason mimay'nei hayeshua.
Mayim, heiy mayim be'sason! Heiy, mayim, b'sason.

Therefore, with joy shall you draw water out of the wells of salvation.
Water with joy! (Isaiah 12:3)

Mi Ohev et HaShabbat

מִי אוֹהֵב אֶת הַשַּׁבָּת? אִמָּא וְאַבָּא!
מִי אוֹהֵב אֶת הַשַּׁבָּת? סָבְתָא וְסַבָּא!
מִי אוֹהֵב אֶת הַשַּׁבָּת? אֲנִי, אַתָּה וְאַתְּ. כָּל הָעוֹלָם כִּמְעַט!
אָז לָמָּה לֹא כָּל יוֹם שַׁבָּת?

Mi oheiv et haShabbat? Ima v'Aba!
Mi oheiv et haShabbat? Savta v'Saba!
Mi oheiv et haShabbat? Ani, atah ve'at. Kal ha-olam ki-m'at!
Az lamah lo kal yom Shabbat?

יוֹם רִאשׁוֹן, שֵׁנִי, שְׁלִישִׁי, כָּל יוֹם נִמְשַׁךְ שָׁנָה
רְבִיעִי אֵת חֲמִישִׁי נוֹתֵן בְּמַתָּנָה.
הַיָּמִים עוֹבְרִים לְאַט רִאשׁוֹן עַד חֲמִישִׁי וּמָחָר מָחָר שַׁבָּת
כִּי בָּא כְּבָר יוֹם שִׁישִׁי!

Yom rishon sheini sh'lishi, kal yom nimshakh shanah
revi'i eit ḥamishi notein bema-tanah.
Hayamim ov'rim l'at rishon ad ḥamishi u-maḥar maḥar Shabbat
ki ba k'var yom shishi!

Who loves the Shabbat? Mommy and Daddy! Who loves the Shabbat? Grandmother and Grandfather! Who loves the Shabbat? Me, you and you. The whole world almost! So why isn't every day a Shabbat?

Sunday, Monday, Tuesday, Every day lasts a year. Wednesday gives Thursday as a gift, the days pass slowly, first to fifth. But tomorrow, tomorrow is the Shabbat, because it's already Friday!

Od Yishama

עוֹד יִשָּׁמַע בְּעָרֵי יְהוּדָה וּבְחוּצוֹת יְרוּשָׁלַיִם
קוֹל שָׂשׂוֹן וְקוֹל שִׂמְחָה, קוֹל חָתָן וְקוֹל כַּלָּה.

Od yishama b'arei Yehudah u'veḥutsot Yerushalayim.
Kol sason v'kol simḥah, kol ḥatan v'kol khalah.

Yet again there shall be heard in the cities of Judah and in the streets of Jerusalem the voice of joy and the voice of gladness, the voice of the bridegroom and the voice of the bride. (Jeremiah 33:10-11)

Oseh Shalom

עוֹשֶׂה שָׁלוֹם בִּמְרוֹמָיו הוּא יַעֲשֶׂה שָׁלוֹם עָלֵינוּ
וְעַל כָּל יִשְׂרָאֵל, וְאִמְרוּ: אָמֵן.

Oseh shalom bimromayv hu ya'aseh shalom aleinu
v'al kal Yisraeil, v'imru: amein.

May He who creates peace in His high heavens, create peace for us and for all Israel, and let us say amen.

Shabbat Shalom

Shabbat Shalom שַׁבָּת שָׁלוֹם

Shalom Ḥaveirim

שָׁלוֹם חֲבֵרִים, שָׁלוֹם חֲבֵרִים שָׁלוֹם, שָׁלוֹם
לְהִתְרָאוֹת, לְהִתְרָאוֹת שָׁלוֹם, שָׁלוֹם

Shalom ḥaveirim, shalom ḥaveirim, shalom, shalom
L'hit-ra'ot, l'hit-ra'ot, shalom, shalom.

Good-bye my friends, until we see you again, shalom.

Siman Tov

סִימָן טוֹב וּמַזָּל טוֹב יְהֵא לָנוּ, וּלְכָל יִשְׂרָאֵל, אָמֵן.

Siman tov u'mazal tov yehei lanu, u'lekhal Yisraeil, amein.

May favor and good luck be with us and all of Israel, amen.

V'haeir Eineinu

וְהָאֵר עֵינֵינוּ בְּתוֹרָתֶךָ, וְדַבֵּק לִבֵּנוּ בְּמִצְוֹתֶיךָ, וְיַחֵד לְבָבֵנוּ
לְאַהֲבָה וּלְיִרְאָה אֶת שְׁמֶךָ. וְלֹא נֵבוֹשׁ לְעוֹלָם וָעֶד.
כִּי בְשֵׁם קָדְשְׁךָ הַגָּדוֹל וְהַנּוֹרָא בָּטָחְנוּ. נָגִילָה וְנִשְׂמְחָה
בִּישׁוּעָתֶךָ.

V'haeir eineinu b'Toratekha, v'dabeik libeinu bemits'votekha, v'yaḥeid liva'veinu, l'ahavah ul'yirah et sh'mekha. V'lo neivosh l'olam va'ed. Ki v'sheim kad'shekha hagadol v'hanora ba'taḥ'nu na'gilah venis'meḥah bi'shua'tekha.

Enlighten our eyes in Your instruction; cause our heart to cleave to Your commandments, and unify our heart to love and to fear Your Name, so we will never be put to shame. In Your holy, great and awesome Name we trusted, that we might thrill with joy in Your salvation.

Yibaneh HaMikdash

יִבָּנֶה הַמִּקְדָּשׁ, עִיר צִיּוֹן תְּמַלֵּא, וְשָׁם נָשִׁיר שִׁיר חָדָשׁ
וּבִרְנָנָה נַעֲלֶה.

Yibaneh haMik'dash, ir Tsiyon timalei, v'sham nashir shir ḥadash u-vir'nanah na'aleh.

Let the Temple be rebuilt, Tsiyon restored,
that we may ascend there singing a new song.

Additional Blessings

Prayer for Travelers

יְהִי רָצוֹן מִלְּפָנֶיךָ יְיָ אֱלֹהֵינוּ וֵאלֹהֵי אֲבוֹתֵינוּ,
שֶׁתּוֹלִיכֵנוּ לְשָׁלוֹם, וְתַצְעִידֵנוּ לְשָׁלוֹם, וְתַדְרִיכֵנוּ לְשָׁלוֹם,
וְתִסְמְכֵנוּ לְשָׁלוֹם, וְתַגִּיעֵנוּ לִמְחוֹז חֶפְצֵנוּ לְחַיִּים וּלְשִׂמְחָה
וּלְשָׁלוֹם. וְתַצִּילֵנוּ מִכַּף כָּל־אוֹיֵב, וְאוֹרֵב וְלִסְטִים וְחַיּוֹת
רָעוֹת בַּדֶּרֶךְ, וּמִכָּל מִינֵי פֻּרְעָנִיּוֹת הַמִּתְרַגְּשׁוֹת לָבוֹא
לָעוֹלָם. וְתִתְּנֵנוּ לְחֵן וּלְחֶסֶד וּלְרַחֲמִים בְּעֵינֶיךָ וּבְעֵינֵי כָל
רֹאֵינוּ. כִּי אֵל שׁוֹמֵעַ תְּפִלָּה וְתַחֲנוּן אָתָּה.
בָּרוּךְ אַתָּה יְיָ, שׁוֹמֵעַ תְּפִלָּה.

Y'hi ratson mil-fanekha Adonai Eloheinu ve-lohei avoteinu, she-tolikheinu l'shalom, v'tats'ideinu l'shalom, v'tad-rikheinu l'shalom, v'tism'kheinu l'shalom, v'tagi'einu limḥoz ḥeftseinu l'ḥayim ul'simḥah ul'shalom. V'tatsileinu mi-kaf kal oyeiv v'oreiv v'listim v'ḥayot ra-ot va-derekh, u-mi-kol min-ei pur'aniyot hamit-rag'shot la-vo la-olam. V'tit'neinu l'ḥein u'leḥesed u'leraḥamim b'einekha uv'einei khal ro-einu. Ki eil sho-mei-a t'filah v'taḥanun atah. Barukh atah Adonai sho-mei'a t'filah.

May it be Your will, Lord, our God and God of our fathers, that You lead us toward peace, guide our footsteps toward peace, and make us reach our desired destination for life, gladness, and peace. May You rescue us from the hand of every foe, ambush along the way, and from all manner of difficulties that might come on our way. May You send blessing in our efforts, and grant us grace, kindness, and mercy in Your eyes and in the eyes of all who see us. May You hear the sound of our humble request because You are God who hears prayer requests. Blessed are You, Lord, who hears prayer.

Blessings before Food or Drink

Beginning of every blessing: בָּרוּךְ אַתָּה יְיָ אֱלֹהֵינוּ מֶלֶךְ הָעוֹלָם...

Barukh atah Adonai Eloheinu Melekh Ha'Olam...

Blessed are You, Lord our God, King of the Universe…

Before eating bread: ...הַמּוֹצִיא לֶחֶם מִן הָאָרֶץ.

...hamotsi leḥem min ha'arets. ...who brings forth bread from the earth.

Before eating food of wheat, barley, rye, oats, or spelt: ...בּוֹרֵא מִינֵי מְזוֹנוֹת.

...borei minei m'zunot. …who creates species of nourishment.

Before drinking grape wine or grape juice: ...בּוֹרֵא פְּרִי הַגָּפֶן.

...borei p'ri ha'gafen. …who creates the fruit of the vine.

Before eating tree-grown fruit: ...בּוֹרֵא פְּרִי הָעֵץ.

...borei p'ri ha'eits. …who creates the fruit of the tree.

Before eating food that grew directly from the earth: ...בּוֹרֵא פְּרִי הָאֲדָמָה.

...borei p'ri ha'adamah. …who creates the fruit of the ground.

Before eating or drinking any other foods: ...שֶׁהַכֹּל נִהְיָה בִּדְבָרוֹ.

...shehakhol ni-heyah bid'varo. …through whose word everything came to be.

Birkat HaMazon - Brief Version

(This very short Birkat follows the traditional minimal requirement to mention the Food, the Land of Israel, Jerusalem's sanctity and G-d's Goodness after eating)

בָּרוּךְ אַתָּה יְיָ, אֱלֹהֵינוּ מֶלֶךְ הָעוֹלָם, הַזָּן אֶת הַכֹּל.
נוֹדֶה לְךָ יְיָ אֱלֹהֵינוּ, עַל הָאָרֶץ וְעַל הַמָּזוֹן.
וּבְנֵה יְרוּשָׁלַיִם עִיר הַקֹּדֶשׁ בִּמְהֵרָה בְיָמֵינוּ.
הַמֶּלֶךְ הַטּוֹב, וְהַמֵּטִיב לַכֹּל. וּמִכָּל טוּב לְעוֹלָם אַל יְחַסְּרֵנוּ.

Barukh atah Adonai, Eloheinu Melekh Ha'Olam, hazan et hakol.
Nodeh l'kha, Adonai Eloheinu, al ha'arets v'al hamazon.
Uv'neih Y'rushalayim ir hakodesh bimheirah v'yameinu.
HaMelekh hatov v'hameitiv lakol. Umikol tov l'olam al y'has'reinu.

Blessed are You, Lord our God, King of the Universe, who provides food for all.
We thank You Lord our God, for the Land and for its produce.
Rebuild Jerusalem as a holy city very soon, even in our day.
The Good King is good to all. May You, who knows our need, always provide us with good.